TOWARDS THE 21ST CENTURY:
DOING THE GOOD

by
BERNHARD J. LIEVEGOED, M.D.

STEINER BOOK CENTRE, INC.
151 Carisbrooke Crescent
North Vancouver, V7N 2S2
Canada

ISBN 0-919924-04-2

First Edition 1972
Reprinted 1974
Reprinted 1979

Edited by Rufus Goodwin from a cycle of lectures given in Spring Valley N.Y. in the summer of 1965 by Professor Bernhard J. Lievegoed, M.D., Director of the Netherlands Pedagogical Institute.

Script unrevised by the author.

Permission to quote from the 'Stages of Higher Knowledge' kindly given by the publisher, Anthroposophic Press Inc., of New York, U.S.A.

(©) Steiner Book Centre

ALL RIGHTS RESERVED

Contents

Publisher's note	v
This century	1
The whirlpool	11
The good	25
Three trials	34
The new morale	44
Group life	56
Systems, levels, threefoldness	66
Towards the 21st century	76

ABOUT THE AUTHOR

Dr. Lievegoed was born in Indonesia in 1905 where he spent his youth. He went to Holland to study medicine at Groningen and Amsterdam and was qualified in 1930, and then followed a year of European orientation in an area hitherto little developed — child psychiatry.

In 1931 he was the leading figure in the founding of a home for curative pedagogy and in 1939 he obtained his Ph.D. with a thesis on Music Therapy from the University of Leiden.

From this phase he was led to a study of pedagogical questions in relation to human beings in industry. In 1954 he was appointed Professor at University of Rotterdam.

While there he founded the Netherlands Pedagogical Insitute which offered assistance to industry to which he makes reference in this book.

The latest phase in Dr. Lievegoed's life was the foundation, with the help of a government grant, of the Free University in 1970 in Driebergen, the aim of which is to enable young people to find a direction in life.

ABOUT THE BOOK

The ideas which led to the Free University were evidently already in Dr. Lievegoed's mind when he gave these talks, for the theme running through them is to point out the young men and women of today the dangers they face and the way to meet them.

Publisher's Note

Because the words 'Imagination', 'Inspiration' and 'Intuition' in this work have a specialized meaning the initial letter has been capitalized. The meaning in each case is explained briefly by excerpts given below from a work by Rudolf Steiner entitled 'The Stages of Higher Knowledge', published by Anthroposophic Press Inc., New York, with permission of Rudolf Steiner Nachlassverwaltung of Dornach, Switzerland.

Ordinary knowledge in a healthy individual creates no image and no concept when an object does not confront the outer senses. The ego then remains inactive. Whoever forms images of which the corresponding sense-objects do not actually exist lives in fantasy. – But the occult student acquires this very faculty of forming images without the stimulus of external sense-objects. With him something else must take the place of outer objects. He must be able to form images although no object touches his senses. Something must step in to replace sensation. This something is *Imagination*. At this stage, images appear to the occult student in exactly the same way as if a sense-object were making an impression upon him: They are as vivid and true as sense-images, yet they are not of material, but of soul-spirit origin. Yet the senses remain entirely inactive. – It is evident that the individual must first acquire this faculty of forming *meaningful images* without sense-impressions. This is accomplished through meditation and through the exercises which have been described in the book, *Knowledge of the Higher Worlds and Its Attainment*. The man confined to the sense-world lives only among images which have reached him through the senses. And now the world of the third stage of knowledge! Nothing in the sense-world can even suggest its wealth and abundance. What was sensation at the first stage of cognition, imagination at the second, here becomes 'inspiration'. Inspiration gives the impressions, and the ego forms the concepts. If anything at all in the realm of sense can be compared with this world of Inspiration, it is the world of tone opened up to us by the sense of hearing. But now not the tones of earthly music are concerned, but purely 'spiritual tones'. One begins to 'hear' what is going on at the heart of things. The stone, the plant, and so forth, become 'spiritual words'. The world begins to express its true nature to the soul. It sounds grotesque, but it is literally true, that at this stage of knowledge one 'hears spiritually the growing of the grass'. The crystal form is perceived like sound; the opening blossom 'speaks' to men. The inspired man is able to proclaim the inner nature of things; everything rises up before his soul, as though from the dead, in a new kind of way. He speaks a language which stems from another world, and which alone can make the every-day world comprehensible.

The actual *living* of things within the soul is Intuition. When it is said of Intuition that 'through it man creeps into all things', this is literally true. – In ordinary life man has only one 'intuition' – namely, of the ego itself. For the ego can in no way be perceived from without; it can only be experienced in the inner life. A simple consideration will make this fact clear. It is a consideration which has not been applied by psychologists with sufficient exactitude. Unimpressive as it may appear, to one with full understanding, it is of the most far-reaching significance. It is as follows: A thing in the outer world can be called by all men by the self-same name. A table can be spoken of by all as a 'table'; a tulip by all as a 'tulip'. Mr. Miller can be addressed by all as 'Mr. Miller'. But there is one word which each can apply only to himself. This is the word 'I'. No other person can call me 'I'. To any one else I am a 'you'. In the same way everyone else is a 'you' to me. Only I can say 'I' to myself. This is because each man lives, not outside, but within the 'I'. And in the same way, in intuitive cognition, one lives in all things. The perception of the ego is the prototype of all intuitive cognition. Thus to enter into all things, one must first step outside oneself. One must become 'selfless' in order to become blended with the 'self', the 'ego' of another being.

This Century

When we ask the question: What is the significance of anthroposophy and the anthroposophical movement in the present world? – we can take two points of view.

One point of view says: anthroposophy is one of the many little sects, of about 30,000 members, without influence on the happenings of the world; a sect, true, which has done some things – for instance, its members have founded schools and they teach children in a queer way.

There is another view. Spiritual reality does not reckon with quantity, but with quality – the quality of consciousness and the quality of will power. One man, thinking spiritual reality on one continent, is a light that radiates throughout the whole continent, just as when a candle is lit in a dark room and light reaches the whole room. When, on a certain continent, or in a big country, one or a few people think spiritual reality, then in a spiritual sense this part of the earth is not dark.

Spirituality, in this sense, is the quality of consciousness, and we can ask, when we speak about anthroposophy today: 'Do we really have the quality of consciousness and the quality of will power which our time needs?' Only absolute honesty and absolute modesty can give the answer.

Until 1500, mankind was led by the Hierarchies. All that happened till 1500 (Rudolf Steiner, the founder of anthroposophy, told this to young teachers of the schools in 1922) were *repetitions of repetitions of repetitions*. What does that mean? It means that all those things which happened in the Greek and Roman culture, and in the Middle Ages, were still a repetition of things which had been brought to the world by the Hierarchies in previous periods. After 1500, said Steiner: 'For the first time in the development of the earth, for the first time since the Saturn epoch, mankind is also responsible for the development and evolution of the universe. For the first time what happens – after 1500 – is not a repetition: it is new.'

This new element is the development of the *consciousness soul*.

Before 1500, in the early post-Atlantean periods, leaders of mankind were inspired by Hierarchical beings. These leaders were the half-gods of the ancient Greeks. Of Gilgamesh, too, it was said that he was one-third man, two-thirds god. That meant he was imbued by a Hierarchical being who acted through this leader as a leading force of mankind. Only after 1500 begins the leadership of man *by man*.

Steiner says that the great leader of the Sun mysteries from Atlantean times, Manu, was 'God-Manu', and that after 1500 there were to come 'human-Manu' – human leaders working out of the spiritual forces of the Sun mysteries.

This transition in 1500 is not recorded by modern history. On earth, for centuries, people have not been able to look into the reality of spiritual worlds. About 1500 the First Hierarchy entered the human world and gave to the physiology of man quite a new impulse. Till then, cosmic intelligence had lived in man and in the hearts of men in a different way. The old texts of the Kalevala or of Homer described gods who were near to men, so near that they went directly into the life of man and spoke to his heart and intelligence through the old mysteries. Knowledge was not only intellectual knowledge. Knowledge was something which filled the whole person and radiated out of the heart forces, something which was so one with man that he did not *have* the knowledge – he *was* the knowledge. It was *in* him – he *had* it not.

The First Hierarchy thus intervened in human development: the capacity to think, to have thoughts, moved from the heart to the brains. That is the starting point of personal intelligence.

The Archangel Michael had been trustee of the cosmic intelligence of the great Sun mysteries. Michael had always been the servant of the Sun mysteries. The old histories and the old sayings of the people record how, at certain points of history, Michael spoke and intervened in destiny. The leader of mankind's real development was always Michael. He incarnated into the leaders of old cultures.

The possibility to think and to have thoughts then moved from the heart, from the whole human being, which it had filled, to the brain – to the head. The intellect developed, and in a new way. Michael, so to speak, withdrew. Intelligence could be produced by human brains, now no longer necessarily inspired. As intelligence came to be produced by human beings, Ahriman could get a grip on human thinking. So long as cosmic thoughts had lived in the hearts of people, Ahriman could not enter. The moment thinking went to the brains, Ahriman could enter and try to capture the thinking of man.

Another thing changed too. In the 19th letter of the *Letters to the Members*, Steiner writes that in nature there is always a surplus of young seed forces. When the plants come up in the spring there are more life forces than are needed for the growing of the plant. These surplus forces, radiating to the cosmos, are the young seed forces for the next cosmic situation, that of the coming Jupiter evolution. This is the situation in nature. After 1500, there is also a surplus in the will power of man, which radiates out along with these young seed forces. In man there is a surplus of will power, radiating into the cosmos, and this, too, will be part of the forces which form new cosmic creations.

Mankind is now co-operating in the creation of the coming worlds with his will forces, either by his spiritual will forces when it is done in a good way, or, in the wrong way, by his materialistic will forces. He is responsible now for what he wills. That is a new aspect of our present situation.

Steiner tells how thinking forces, in a sense, have died. They are shadows of thinking that lived in an earlier age. Even when we think about the reality of Saturn, Sun, Moon, and Earth development, all this remains dead when we know it only with our heads.

But will forces are a path for the earth's new upspringing life. Only where, knowing about spiritual realities and thinking about them, they engage the will, only then do these thoughts take on life.

Steiner put this in one sentence: 'The past, casting shadows, and the future, holding seeds of new reality, meet together in the being of man. Their meeting is the real human life of the present.'

There can, of course, be aberrations: one of only thinking and knowing; another of only willing, but having no spiritual content. Only where the spiritual content enters the will is the real human life of the present working. So we understand that mankind is now co-operating in the creation of the coming worlds through spiritual will forces. With our heads we can think spiritual conceptions, but from our heads these conceptions must enter into the will. And when I speak about the real situation of today, I would say: We must learn to *will*, to *will* in a spiritual way, to *will* with a spiritual content. What counts for the future of mankind is what we will, not the success of the action. The will is what counts – the surplus of will forces as they radiate out into the cosmos. They become the seed forces for new worlds.

After 1500, Michael withdrew from mankind. He no longer held the connection with those thoughts which were produced by human brains, but he began to prepare for his coming in 1879 as the Time Spirit. This he did, preparing his mission in a cosmic school, where he once again brought great imaginations to those souls not yet incarnated but which would be on earth at the end of the 19th and during the 20th century. Once again he taught cosmic intelligence, for which he had been the trustee since Atlantean times. And it was the content of this school which Steiner introduced through anthroposophy.

Steiner, one of the leaders working out of the central forces of the mysteries of the Sun, had the task of introducing this cosmic intelligence on earth in the 20th century, in human words, and in human thinking, so that it might inspire human feeling and human willing.

Anthroposophy was presented first in the form of philosophy, as a way of inner development, and as a cosmology. Later it added insight into the New Testament, the four Gospels, and, after the First World War, the Michael wisdom was moulded into a school of esoteric learning as well. So we see:

1879 Michael takes up his task as the Time Spirit.
1899 the end of 5,000 years of darkness, of Kali-Yuga.
1900 beginning of a period of new light, a period when spiritual light could again flow to the earth.

We can observe Rudolf Steiner introducing this cosmic intelligence to the world in three steps – in three seven-year periods. Over the first period, from 1902–1909, Steiner introduces his *Philosophy of Freedom*, his *Knowledge of the Higher Worlds* (which is the way of inner development), and *Theosophy*. This period ends with *Occult Science*, outlining the whole cosmology of our world.

From 1909–1916, the arts were developed – the renewal of movement in eurythmy, speech, and drama. In a short time Steiner wrote his four mystery dramas. He also threw new light on the four Gospels.

In 1917, Steiner introduced his concepts of the threefold form of man, and from 1917–1923 he worked out the structure of the threefold social order.

During the first seven years, anthroposophy was placed before the members as a great Imagination. For the second seven years anthroposophy was placed before the feeling forces, which could develop in art and in a renewal of religion.

In the third seven years Steiner reached into the will life to found a new education, new schools, a new movement for medicine, a new movement for bio-dynamic farming, and a new movement of the Threefold Commonwealth for social life.

At the end of 1923, it was possible for Steiner to celebrate the Christmas Foundation ceremony for the Anthroposophical Society, and in the Christmas Foundation, he introduced the renewed mysteries. That is to say, he introduced these mysteries into people's will. He then said: 'I myself, now, will go into this. I will join the Executive Committee, and I will take the chair. The Executive Committee will be a body for doing, for action, and for spiritual insight.' An initiative group, in other words: that means things had to be done – not only known, not only felt. Things have to be known, felt, and *done*.

This was the span of Rudolf Steiner's life in this century, as seen in retrospect.

Such seven-year rhythms live in the development of anthroposophy as a whole. There are such rhythms throughout cosmic development – the rhythm of day and night, of the year, of the sun passing through the zodiac. They are all rhythms written into the universe by the working of spiritual Hierarchies in past times of evolution. Now there is one new rhythm of development. That is the rhythm of $33\frac{1}{3}$ years – the rhythm between Christmas and the Easter that comes $33\frac{1}{3}$ years later. This is a new rhythm in the cosmos, a rhythm which was written by the life of Christ on earth. The life of Christ on earth meant that from that moment on, when Christ died at the first Easter, the rhythm of $33\frac{1}{3}$ years became a rhythm connected with all real Christian development. The old rhythms of days, years, and centuries are all realities, but new reality intersected earth life, caused by the life of Christ. Steiner, in one of his lectures, says that when something is done in the world and a new impulse is born, it is Christmas morning for this impulse. Then $33\frac{1}{3}$ years later, this impulse will have its Easter and its resurrection.

Whoever knows about this can find in his own life, and in the happenings of social life, the secret rhythm of $33\frac{1}{3}$ years. It works where the impulse is connected with the impulses of Christ working on the development of mankind.

We can note in this century, perhaps more than in previous times, the working of this rhythm. Steiner speaks of this: of the last third of the 19th century, and of the first third of the 20th century. Remember, 1900 began the new epoch of light. Kali-Yuga had ended. New light could flow to the earth. Steiner, in 1899, went through inner realities which gave him the possibility, and the task, of entering into the new century to introduce the imaginations of the Michael school as it had worked spiritually from 1500 onwards.

Now we can ask: 'What was the task of the new time, the 20th century, the beginning of the century of light?'

For one thing, that anthroposophy *as a whole* and I take it now as a whole – should be introduced to mankind. Anthroposophy – a body of wisdom. We can say the seed was introduced of a new philosophy, a new science, a new art, and of a new religious renewal. These were seeds of new ways of inner development, seeds for the beginnings of new mysteries. This wisdom had to be studied. The small group which was with Rudolf Steiner was, of course, led not only by this wisdom; Lucifer tried to pervade this group also. Lucifer whispered to the members: 'You are the happy few. You know the truth. Shut yourselves away from the evil world. Study, and study for your *own* development and satisfaction.' This is the classic Luciferic approach. Anthroposophists versus *the outside world*. This expression, *the outside world*, is Luciferic jargon.

At Easter, 1933, the second third of the 20th century began. What was the greatest event of this second period? In 1911 and 1912 Steiner spoke about this great happening. He said that Christ had undergone a new crucifixion through the materialism of the 19th century. The materialism of the 19th century meant such suffering for Christ that it was for him a new crucifixion. Steiner also said that Christ would have a resurrection in the etheric world and appear as the etheric Christ between 1933 and 1935, and from then on, for future times. The appearance of the etheric Christ was the thing which had to happen in the middle third of this 20th century. People should be aware of it, should be prepared to encounter this happening. Now we realize how the forces of darkness did all they could to steer the minds of people on other paths. Shortly before this time, in January 1933, Hitler came to power. That is what happened; we know the results. They all stared at this man: 'What is happening?' 'What is he doing?' It was impossible then for people to go through what was really happening in the world. The real happening was not in Germany at the beginning of 1933; what was really happening was that the etheric Christ was coming to mankind.

Can we, through Steiner, prepare to find the way to the etheric Christ? Steiner describes this preparation, saying that there are three steps which man must first go through, not only as knowledge, but in feeling – such strong inner feeling that man *becomes* this feeling. The first feeling is of the worthlessness of outer human existence. The second is the feeling of dissatisfaction with materialistic explanations. When we have studied anthroposophy for a long enough time, we may be deeply satisfied with the explanations given by anthroposophy. But this must be deepened more and more. Then the third step: the feeling of an inner split, inner duality. The feeling: 'My cosmic being, my cosmic ego, is great and radiant, while on earth I am only a dwarf. I am a cripple who cannot appear as my true being.' Steiner said the question arises in us: 'Who is posing me my own riddles? My own cosmic being, my own true ego!'

When people have gone through this deep dissatisfaction with all that is the outer world, it can result, Steiner said, in a new morality. The new morality is universal pity, compassion with all that suffers. He said that we should not be able to sleep at night so long as there is suffering in the world. Yet many of us have slept well many nights since.

Steiner said Christ would speak out of the grey depths of the spirit. Out of the grey depths of the spirit Christ would speak words of consolation. To be able to hear words of consolation, however, we must have a need to be consoled. The fact is that our normal outer feelings need no consoling. To feel this need we must have gone through the experience of the new morality: feel this universal pity, this compassion with all that suffers.

It was the task in the middle of our own century, as I see it, for anthroposophy to develop into a broad open movement reaching into the world, knowing about the world – not only with the head, but with the heart. Just as the study of anthroposophy means developing the quality of Imagination, so going through this deep feeling for the world, with an open mind, brings the real forces of Inspiration. Through anthroposophy in the second part of this century, a great many people should develop forces of Inspiration.

It is my opinion that we, and I say we, as a whole, have so far failed in this mission. We had not the force to be really awake in that darkness to come to the etheric kingdom and to find there the Christ. Can anything be done now? In that time when all the forces of anthroposophy were to be awakened in the inner heart so that the etheric Christ could find people through whom to speak and work in the world, we went our egotistic ways. We fought and quarrelled with each other about books and about right methods. I am deeply ashamed when I look back upon this period. I must say all of us who were then in anthroposophy were involved, and we hadn't that force in us to really see what was happening in the world, and what was the task of the middle part of this century. Perhaps we can still do something. We can perhaps try to set aside egotistic quarrelling, living with our soul as an ear to the world, listening to people as we listen to a work of art, to a symphony or to a piece of Bach, so that that which is behind people reveals itself. And we can try to give answers out of our own compassion and our sympathy with the people of the world.

At Michaelmas 1966, we were entering the third and last part of the century. We can ask what will be the task of anthroposophy and of the people who could know, through it, about this last third of the century? Having studied anthroposophy as a cosmic wisdom, and having come to some Imagination, we can think through Steiner: 'When I can think through the cosmic development from Saturn to Sun to Moon to Earth, I am already in the world of Imagination, because these are pictures not taken from something that could be seen. They are inner pictures, and all inner pictures are the beginning of Imagination.'

We can live through a second step and try to come to Inspiration by living with people and with the world, receiving perhaps some consolation by way of Intuition. Through this we may know what to do in the encounter with Ahriman, and how to create young seed forces for the future. Steiner has told us that this last part of the century will be a very severe and difficult one. Ahriman will try to cast aside everything connected with spiritual science and with spiritual knowledge, and we will have to try to find the way in the world out of our own being.

Ahriman will try to eliminate the freedom of will given by the gods after 1500. Ahriman is preparing. He tries to eliminate the free will, and he does it in very clever ways. He does it by data processing, as we call it, by working with mechanical information, by research operations, and things like that.

What he is doing is trying to collect information and then

make a short cut from information to decision. He wants to tell us that, when such and such is the information, then we can only do this and that; all other ways are wrong.

But really coming to a decision means that we have to have Imagination, also for ourselves. *We* have to get the information, which means that we make a picture of the reality that we have to deal with. Then we have to develop consideration or sound judgement, which is an Inspirational force. *Then* we must come to a decision, already partly Intuition. It is in this middle step of sound judgement, of consideration, that the human being can be creative.

Creativity means that all things brought to us as information, as data, as facts, have to be interpreted and considered anew by our deepest forces. We have to take our decisions out of the conditions given at that moment. Then only will our judgement be strong enough to withstand Ahriman – when it comes of Inspiration, out of the spirit. Out of the spirit means for us out of the forces of the etheric Christ, who speaks words of consolation in the depths of our soul. Only now can that Intuition reach the will *for the deed*. When it does, we shall know what to do in the social field in which we are working and living.

In the last part of our century we have to enter these mysteries of the will.

We can live out of Intuition when we live as a group of people who are working together to accomplish an objective in the world. It can be a school, it can be an institute, it can be a farm. Steiner spoke of this in 1924, in the lectures which he held in Torquay, England, about initiate consciousness. He spoke about two ways of initiation: the old and the new way. The new way of initiation is that of Intuition, Intuition which can be found in a group of people who are working together. Steiner says that such a group must be a karmic group. Karma, not only from the past, but, as can also be the case, karma for the future. We build up a karmic group of people, with whom we were never together before, when together with these people we *will* something.

When such an Intuition springs up in a group of people working out of anthroposophy in the world, they must bring their good qualities and positive possibilities into the work, withdrawing their negative side from the group work. That negative side they must take into themselves and fight with in the loneliness of their own life. They must make the sacrifice of not bringing the negative, personal things into the group work. This is a very difficult thing. The working group which is able to do this, even for only a short time, is able to live out of Intuition; it brings into the world those forces of germinating will which go into the future.

We shall have to do this, because we shall have to meet Ahriman in his own incarnation around the year 2,000. Steiner told us, in the last year of his life, that the great Aristotelians, Steiner himself included, would be back at this time. They will be able to give another direction to science. They will work together with the great Platonists, who are people of enormous will for the good in social life. Platonists are not people with feeble wills, and where this will is, it will be a will for good in the social life.

In this next, last part of the century, we must be able *to do* that which is good. We can know the truth and what is right. But knowing what is right is not the same as doing what is good. Something which is really truth to someone can be very bad at one moment, because the good is always relative, bound to a certain time, to certain environment.

In 1902 Steiner said in *Knowledge of the Higher Worlds* that one of the things we have to develop further is spiritual tact. With this spiritual tact we have to work in the coming years, doing the good according to the situations which we meet.

That doesn't mean in isolation and alone, but in social life, with other people.

The Whirlpool

The 20th century is a divided century. Kali-Yuga ended in 1899. New light could flow to earth. On the other hand, this is a century of darkness in the extreme. Where there is light, there are shadows. When we see the darkness of the shadows, we remember that they come from a very bright light.

The last part of this century, which began at Michaelmas 1966, will be dramatic. The battle between Michael light forces on one side, and the Ahrimanic forces on the other, will reach an extreme climax. In the Bible, the Revelations of St. John say: '. . . the devil worked and worked and worked, knowing that he had a short time.'

When I look upon what is happening now, behind the curtains of the physical world, I remember a personal letter Steiner wrote. I had the opportunity to read it and see how Steiner described the spiritual situation of this age. He painted a picture for the eye of the Imagination, saying: Ahriman sits in a cave under the ground. He ciphers and figures and counts, doing it with the greatest intensity. Michael stands behind him, sword in hand, while in the cave under the ground, Ahriman figures and ciphers, trying to solve everything by organization, in his way, with an awful force of intellect. Giving him his time, Michael knows that he shall do the addition.

This picture helps us realize that, although things will be very difficult in the years towards the end of the century, there will be help from the side of light.

Now we have read in the work of Steiner how, at the end of the last third of the century, the whole Michael School will come to earth. The great personalities out of the school of Chartres and the great personalities out of the Dominican movement will all come to earth and work together. These two streams of very powerful souls who have not yet worked together on earth will meet here for the first time. The great individualities of the school of Chartres will take part, and since they are Platonists, they will work with great will power in the field of art, in the social field, and in the field of philosophy and thinking. They will work with such a power that they will add new forces to balance what is coming out of the school of Ahriman.

Steiner says that he who fights for Michael in the coming years will come into a whirlpool of Ahrimanic, Luciferic and Michaelic forces. This whirlpool will be of such an intensity that it will not be easy to know, in any given moment: 'Where am I standing, and for what am I working?' It needs very great insight into the things you are doing. Perhaps we think, 'Now I am really working for anthroposophy, for the spiritual work', yet in that moment we are already in the hands of Lucifer. Perhaps we think, 'Now I am going too deep into the way of science', yet perhaps at that moment we are fighting Ahriman in the right way. We have to be very careful, and I think that many things which are to be done, must be done out of the force of the heart's courage – the courage of going *into* it, doing that which is at hand. Things which people ask of us also give us the possibility of doing. Only afterwards will it be seen whether what was done was good or not.

On one side works the light, on the other works Ahriman. For each new thing that comes from the world of light, Ahriman has a counter-attack. In 1912, Niels Bohr of Copenhagen showed for the first time the model of the atom. I was a student at the beginning of the 1920s and I read a book by the British physicist, Sir Arthur Stanley Eddington, who wrote: 'As Niels Bohr showed me his model of the atom, I had to ask myself, did he *find* the atom or did he *create* the atom?'

I have puzzled over this for years. What does Eddington mean by this question? As a good student of physics my thought was, of course, that Niels Bohr had *found the reality* of the atom. How could a man like Eddington be so silly as to ask: 'Had he found it, or did he create it?' This was a question that might have been put by Steiner. It is a very deep question, and we see how the really great physicists are modest people, people who know the boundaries.

Outstanding physicists seek to be true and clear. They will not go farther than a model of thinking seen only as a model, not as a reality. A second echelon man, however, will speak about the same thing as a reality. That is Ahriman's trick. The outstanding physicists know where they stand. They do not speculate beyond what they can be responsible for. But their assistants speak about the same things as realities, and they react in a not-so-friendly way when reminded of the boundaries of their own conceptions. They get angry.

Ahriman tricks his way into the field of science by possessing these thought models. It is Ahriman's way to build up and possess man-made thought models. The model of the atom is a thought model, man-made.

The first great models found were in chemistry when they tried to find out how atoms were arranged in the molecule. Friedrich August Kekule was the man who found the model of the benzene ring. Much can be learned about how Ahriman inspires people from the way it was found. For years and years Kekule was seeking to understand this. He was once at a congress in London, when, sitting on the upper level of a horse-drawn London bus, going a long distance in the hot summer, he fell asleep. He had a dream of a great festival of black gentlemen clad in medieval costumes, and white ladies dancing. At a certain moment, six black gentlemen formed a ring. The others circled around. At that moment Kekule awoke and knew: 'That is the ring; now I have found it!'

This example is revealing because Steiner says the inspirations of Ahriman always come when the consciousness is lowered.

Another example tells how a man solved a difficult problem in electronics while he was sick with flu. After taking three aspirins and a lemonade, he went to bed with a notebook and pencil, asking to be left alone. He came to the final solution of his problem there and worked it backwards to the beginning. He was sick for three days, then took his notes to the lab where the figures were checked out to see whether they were correct. They were.

Another scientist has said: 'I get my best conceptions when I am tired at the end of the day. I lie down on my couch, think of nothing, and in one moment the whole invention is there.' That is the way, out of the school of Ahriman, things come to people. They are thinking in patterns. That is the way Ahriman wants to build a new world, out of the thought patterns of man. Ahriman wants to bring his thoughts into the heads of men so that they build with these patterns a new man-made world which is not a world of nature, not a world of the future – not of the real development of the future – but a world which stands autonomous as a technical world.

About three months before Bohr made the first announcement

of his atom model, Steiner gave a lecture on *The Etherization of the Blood* and spoke about the coming of the etheric Christ. At the same moment as this model of the atom was formed, Steiner spoke of the coming of the etheric Christ to mankind. He said it would begin between 1933 and 1935, and from then on continue into the next thousands of years.

Ahriman's first step is to try to rearrange nature in man-made models. Also in psychology, man's model is being rearranged. In the United States, in stimulus response psychology, the psychologists see man as an input/output model, as they call it. An input/output model is one in which things go in, are changed and come out again. The output, that which comes out, is changed – but it has the same quantity as what went in. The model itself takes or adds nothing. These psychologists see mankind as an input/output model, and they say that the so-called stimulus response psychology shows how things come into man through the eyes and ears, through the senses. Then things come out. He reacts. This action and reaction is the only activity of man, they say.

In the second part of our century we go a step further. Out of the thought model of the atom, man-made models get built as reality. Command of atomic forces means that we have not only atom bombs but also, now, atomic power plants, plants which give us new power out of atomic forces. That means that what was *thought* in the first part of our century has now been mastered and can be used.

There are also new models of thinking in the field of electronics. A really new model was introduced in the middle third of the 20th century: the feedback model. They call it the homeostatic model. It is a group of forces which stands in equilibrium in itself. When things come at it from outside, it remains not only in balance with itself but also in balance with the surroundings. Such a homeo-static model is used in electronics for new circuits; it makes machines for calculating and automation control.

The thought of feedback was developed so that that which was done out of the homeo-static model to the environment would result in the environment giving something back, thus stabilizing the working of the model.

By 1935 we came far with technical development, but things were mainly aimed at reproducing the movements of the skeleton and the muscles. Since then it has become possible to imitate the workings of the nervous system. Through this comes a new control over machines. With the incorporation of a pattern of the nervous system into the machine, Ahriman could make his next step – machines which are controlled in themselves, foolproof, and automatic. They are no longer dependent on human control. This step made possible a flood of new inventions.

Historically, in the field of electronics, the really new findings came, say, in 1904, 1912, 1920. About every six, eight, or nine years came a really new invention. But over recent years, new fields – new fields which haven't existed before – appear each half year.

We speak about the half-time of certain matter. In half the time, say after 300 years, the radioactivity of a certain material is halved. So we may speak about the half-time of modern sciences. The latest figures are that the half-time of electronics is three to four years, which means that someone qualifying as an engineer in electronics must expect that after three or four years half of what he has learned is obsolete and must be relearned. In mechanical engineering the span is about 10 years. New things are coming with growing rapidity. There is a stream of intellectual thinking, a stream of inventions, pouring into the bright brains of certain young people, which puts electronics in command.

A field of increasing importance is that of bio-chemistry. Bio-chemistry is the field where through the protein molecule the scientists are trying to find what they call the genetic code – information on genetic forces. It is written about weekly. Today everyone hears that genetic forces are dependent only on the building up of molecules of protein in which certain molecules are spread around in a certain way. All the genetic particularities of a person are there in a physical code, they say. That is a thought, a model. And already they talk about getting these genetic forces under control.

In 1964 there was a conference in London with six Nobel Prize winners attending. Of the six, five were American Nobel Prize winners in the field of bio-chemistry. They said that within ten to fifteen years we shall be able to change the genetic formula of men by way of chemical drugs. Then, they said, would come the greatest moment for mankind. We could change mankind and endow it with all the favourable conditions wanted and needed. A journalist had been invited to the group and he asked:

'What is your idea of how you would like to make people?' They looked around and said: 'Well, just as we are.' That is their vision of mankind.

Just as we are means that their vision for mankind is the Nobel Prize winner. They want to change everyone so that he is a possible Nobel Prize winner. When everyone is on that level, they will have to make super Nobel Prize winners. This is a real Ahrimanic imagination in very bright people in the field of biochemistry.

Another conception has arisen in recent times. People speak about homeo-static systems. One cell is a homeo-static system; the circuit of eye to brain to moving finger is a homeo-static system. These systems are in themselves closed and in equilibrium. Then there are forces which are of another kind than the forces which are working in the system – forces which work from outside the system and which disturb the system. They are called *parameters*. Parameters are forces from outside.

In a discussion once which lasted eight to nine weeks, which I had with a group of physicians, electronic specialists, and some people of social science, all together, I asked: 'Please give me an example of a parameter which I can understand.'

A physician answered: 'I shall give you one. In the whole stimulus response conception of the human being there is a factor called motivation; motivation is a parameter to this system. It disturbs the system. It comes out of another world.'

Here we have something wonderful with which we can understand many things of anthroposophy. When speaking with a scientist, and he asks, 'What are the etheric forces?' Just say: 'They are a parameter in the field of physical forces.'

Psychological forces are parameters in the field of living forces. The ego is a parameter in the field of the psychological. This means out of another world, out of another field of forces, out of another quality. Ahriman will be concerned. He doesn't like parameters. Since he doesn't like them, he always tries to incorporate them into the field for which the model is designed.

Let us say we are now in the field of economics. There is a group of young economists who are thinking about the question, 'How much money must we put into Nigeria to prepare there a thousand students of medicine within fifteen years? How much money do we have to put in to have lower schools, middle schools, and medical universities, that I may have so many medical people, so many engineers, and so on?' While they are pondering about that, they are trying to look at a great number of factors, but all those factors have to be reduced to dollars. How much does it cost? What must be invested the first, the second, the third, the fourth, and the fifth year? Then what do they do? They look at the investments in education in Europe and in the United States during the last hundred years. They see that, after having invested so and so much, and figuring it out to a dollar value, then the input was so much investment and the output was so many people on this level, so many people on that level, so many people on another level. They make an average of the last hundred years. Then they say they have a measurement for knowing the input/output model of investing money for educational things in an underdeveloped country.

After these people had done this, they came to me and asked a question: 'We have some parameters in this field. We have heard, and perhaps you know more about it, that in Europe and the United States such investment had already something upon which to work. So we thought we could say the output will be 40 per cent of the average of the last hundred years in the United States. Then we thought we would be closer to the true situation.'

'But,' they added, 'we see when we try it out that we have cases where we put money in and nothing comes out. There must be parameters.'

I said: 'Yes, and I know one of the parameters. I have grown up in Asia. There, when a person in a culture which hasn't adopted the western mind gets education and is graduated from a high school, he is an intellectual. He puts on dark spectacles and takes a fountain pen in his hand. He is an intellectual and he doesn't work. You don't work when you are an intellectual.'

'You know,' I said to them, 'you can put in money. But what gives you the certainty that when they have their degree as a doctor, they will *work* as a doctor? That they will work as a doctor not only in a beautiful hospital in the capital, but also as a doctor in the field, going back to the tribes and trying to do work we expect them to do?'

They said: 'Yes, we understand that and we know it. We have seen examples of it, so now tell us, how much will it cost to accomplish what we want?'

I said: 'It *costs* nothing. But you have to send *people*, people who will *really do* the job.'

There is another field developing now, the field of information finding and of information processing in social life and in business life – system analysis, which tries to sense the pattern of what is going on in groups of people who are working together. It can be a church, it can be a company, it can be a state bureau, it can be an office, a post office, or whatever you like. Can we know exactly how the system works? What are the streams going through it, and so on? This is something right in keeping with the consciousness soul time. The consciousness soul wants to work not by feeling but by really consciously knowing things.

But the difficulty is that such a system is formularized to be put into a machine. That wouldn't be much in itself to worry about, except that these people who do system analysis are trying to go from information directly to decision. They get information; they put it in the model; out of the model comes the answer. This answer should be the decision.

But this answer is only an answer with which you can do something when you know what the criteria are which have been put previously into the model. Then we can look back and say: 'Oh, with this and that criteria, we have found this and that.' But we must know for ourselves the criteria we are using for this moment for this case. When we do that, this whole business of research can be of great help. But most people haven't the time or the insight, and things are getting so complicated that they can only be handled by specialists. The people who have to make the decisions are not able to see the criteria which are built into the model. Yes, great decisions are made today in this way – decisions of foreign affairs, of war and peace, and of economy.

Since atomic forces have come under control, there is in principle no longer any scarcity of energy, and no scarcity of raw materials. If something like wool should run out, we just make something usable in the same way. The modern chemical industry is giving us materials which we were asking before from nature, when we were dependent on nature. This independence from nature is one of the new situations in which we live.

We are already in a state where what were discovered as models in the first third of our century have come under control in the second third. We can ask, what will be coming next? Ahriman is dreaming of conquering, not only the earth, but the universe. He will build his own man-made world, which he will take for himself – away from the evolution of mankind and the evolution of the cosmos. Will he do it? Does he want to do it?

He wants to do it; he will try to do it; and he is on the way to doing it.

But in the back of our minds remains the beautiful Imagination of Michael standing behind, making the additions.

Scientists will soon be in command of the genetic forces of man. People will do all they can to better heredity. When you think of the people who are now speaking about it, and I know one man working in this field, you see it is an awfully clever man, but when you speak to him, you have the feeling you are speaking to a boy of fifteen and not older. He is just like a boy of fifteen to sixteen in his development – a boy with clever, very clever thoughts. He is about forty really, but in his life development, his whole way of standing humanly in life, he is just like an adolescent, with all the enthusiasm which adolescents have and all the negative things adolescents have, as they fight that which they don't like. Now we have to see whether we can do anything against this. Working against something is very difficult when you must be as clever as the opposition.

Steiner asked: Why try to have a logical fight with someone whose logic is other than your own?

Anthroposophists have another logic, but we have to enter the logic of the others and fight them within the field of their logic. Our logic is a parameter to *their* logic, and that means that it is very difficult to find ways. It must be mostly in the purely human field, where you have the opportunity to meet such people. It is possible they come to you, late in an evening. I remember one such time. It was while driving late at night in a car with about 200 miles ahead of us, on a lonely way, no other cars, and then such a man said to me in the darkness of the car: 'You know, when I was twenty-eight years old, I had an experience – an experience which I couldn't understand. About twelve years later, I was in Asia and met an inhabitant there. He looked at me and said: "About twelve years ago, you have experienced this and that." He told me what it was and continued: "I will explain to you what you experienced."'

That Asian man told him what he had experienced twelve years before, which he could see in the man. This was the second experience of the man, and he asked me: 'Now, I hear you are an anthroposophist. Tell me, what is the truth about all this?' So his mind opened, in the night, in a car going about eighty miles an hour, and I could speak for an hour. The next day I met him on the campus. His mind was closed again. But there will come another moment when one can speak with him. People have many more experiences than we know. Just such people as outstanding scientists have inner experiences which they can't share.

One of the things humanity will meet in the next years is more and more steering of the social life through systems analysis. We shall see a total disappearance of the last privacy of men. That is already beginning in Europe. I don't know about here in the States, but in Holland, in the field of medicine, you get a chart at your birth, and on this chart, which goes to a central office in Holland, all your illnesses and everything goes on it.

In the future, then, a doctor who sees a patient just has to phone and get an electronic response to his question from the files. They want to know all about you. This is what will come in the next years: more and more loss of the last privacy. All the things you do will be put down; when you ask why, well it could be of use. At the moment in Holland they are making these records for all hospitalization and medical care. They go to a central office of the department of health, and there they are taken, put down, and worked statistically. Then they say, 'Gall-bladder operation; seventeen days of hospitalization.'

Now suppose there is a surgeon who treats his patients in a different way. Statistically his patients rest for twenty-three days, because he lets them rest a little differently. Not, perhaps, after the first, but after the tenth patient he will get a notification saying: 'Dr. So-and-so, your patients with gall-bladder are staying in the hospital too long; you have to put them out five days earlier.' This is coming more and more into the field of our social life.

What will come in the next years? Abundance. Abundancy of energy, of raw material, of information, of medicine, of food, of clothes, of everything. All this Ahriman wishes to give us. There is only one thing that is prohibited: PERSONAL JUDGEMENT. Ego judgement has to be stamped out.

Ahriman's question is, 'Will cleverness or stupidity prevail?' That's what Rudolf Steiner indicated.

Stupidity, to Ahriman, is all that which comes out of the spiritual world. Another comment of Steiner's was: 'If ever we let ourselves in for a discussion with Ahriman, we should inevitably be shattered by the logical conclusiveness of that certainty of aim with which he manipulates his arguments.'

Ahriman calls *stupidity* everything that does not possess a certain personal intellectuality. Every Ahrimanic being is highly endowed with personal intellect in the way I have now described;

critical, repudiating all things illogical, scornful and contemptuous. When we have Ahriman before us in this way, we shall feel the great contrast between Ahriman and Michael. Michael is not in the least concerned with the *personal* quality of intellect. Only men are tempted to make intelligence *personal*, after the pattern of Ahriman.

Ahriman has a most contemptuous judgement of Michael. He thinks Michael foolish and stupid. For Michael only wills, and has willed through the thousands of years, nay through the aeons, to administer the cosmic-intelligence. Now once again men have the possibility of reaching the intelligence administered by Michael, as something belonging to all mankind, as the common and universal intelligence which benefits all men alike.

That is the great difference between the Michaelic intelligence and the Ahrimanic intellect. Michaelic intelligence benefits all men alike. That means that it is not *my* intellect which *I* possess and with which I can make money. With such intellect you can make much money. You will be enslaved in that same moment. Michael gives a pan-intelligence, that is to say, the cosmic intelligence. This cosmic intelligence of Michael, and of anthroposophy, is to be *given away* to all – to the benefit of all in equal measure. It is to be spoken away, given away, and not to be personal. It can best be brought to people when they are together and try to help each other in it.

How can we in this last part of the century help Michael to get inside the Ahrimanic forces? The only way we can defeat Ahriman is from inside. Inside, in so far that we see what he is doing. As we are trying to work out of anthroposophy we cannot stand outside. We have to go into all things. We have to know how our social life is manipulated, because only by knowing how this is done can we defeat Ahriman. That is the reason why we can't stand alone and have that feeling of *we happy few* and the *bad outside world*.

We can only help Michael in two ways. We have the inner way, which Steiner describes in the beginning of the anthroposophical movement in the book *Knowledge of the Higher Worlds*. Then we have the other way, when we are studying the revelations out of the spiritual world and, by studying, begin our first steps on the way to Imagination.

We go our way of inner development and try, by imitation, to develop our Imagination until we have real pictures of spiritual reality. This Imagination, this picture of spiritual reality, is a counter picture to the Ahrimanic model. Ahriman tries to make imaginations, but in the form of models. We must find the other side of imaginations – go to the real Imagination. We must strengthen the force of Imagination and come to the world of Inspiration, where the picture gets more and more and more real. Out of this spiritual reality in which we then stand we come to the world of Intuition – the realm of ability to do things with spiritual forces. This is the way to look at the world, by going inside, building up an inner world of Imagination, Inspiration, and Intuition.

After the Chrismas Foundation meeting in 1923, Steiner said: 'Now for the first time there can be a second way for mankind. This is the way of the natural sciences.' It is the way Goethe began in his plant studies, looking at the world in such a way that the forces working in the world will be transparent. This is the way of looking through and seeing the reality behind the outer world.

But this is a way on which a man cannot go very far alone. He can make his own first steps, but when he has started, Steiner says, then he should have the help of another, of others, and he should be one of a group which is working together. Not, Steiner says, in order to have the result of our work, the coming to the realities, but so that we may describe them in such a way that they may be brought to other people. That's quite another thing.

I know – but can I bring it to others?

There is a way in which we can go alone, and it is the way that was given in the beginning of the anthroposophical movement. This way is *always* to be taken by everyone in his own inner development, beginning with Imagination, coming to Inspiration, and at last to Intuition. But, Steiner points out, that *now* it is possible to go another way: beginning with Intuition, coming to Inspiration, and lastly to Imagination. We *do* things out of a spiritual certainty. This is a right thing. In doing it, we live with the reality of spiritual forces and, afterwards, we see whether it was good or not. The knowing comes later.

The first was the way of the old mysteries for thousands of years, and the way that had to be gone until 1923. Then Steiner renewed the mysteries and gave this new way. He even said he was hated by people who knew only of the other way. They would say, 'That is the way of irresponsibility. You must first know, then stand in reality, then do.'

Now there come new people, and they say, 'We are working together, and out of our standing in the reality of a group which has an objective *outside* the group – such as a school, a farm, or funds for a new building – we have to *do*.' When they sit together, trying to rely on each other and to work with each other, the moment comes when they have to do. Then it is possible that the right thing can be done out of spiritual certainty, out of Intuition.

Steiner says this is especially possible for a great deal of work in the medical profession. When a doctor stands before patients and they come to him, he has the knowledge of the plants and minerals and of what can be done. Then he must study the people, asking the patient about his troubles. Out of this must come the intuition: 'I have to give him Arnica D-12.'

That is an act of Intuition between two people. Perhaps afterwards he can do it in another way. When I began with my medical work, there was no other place in the world where we could learn about these ways, so I went to the Alrlesheim clinic and asked the doctors, 'What do you give in this and that case?' I had a little booklet. I wrote down all the things that I heard. I had a little booklet with about thirty illnesses and about thirty medicaments. With that I began. I never had such success as that first half year.

What weaves between one who is asking and another who is willing to listen, and to give out of his knowledge, brings the moment when we give the right medicine. Give it, take it – it is right. Afterwards we say to ourselves, 'Why did I give it in this potency?' When we think, we shall find a reason. We can say afterwards, 'Yes, it is reasonable that I did so.'

It is the same between a teacher and a child. While a teacher is in a class, the child may say something which is not reasonable. What has a teacher to do? If he says, 'I must think over the entirety of what Rudolf Steiner said,' it will be too late. He has to *do*. In the evening when he looks back on the day, he will see that he did the right thing or the wrong thing. His Intuition was right or wrong. This Intuition can be a new way of inner development. It has to be *done*. When a school has, say, ten classes with ten class teachers, they are working together out of anthroposophy, spiritually. They are trying to do the best they can, with the works of Steiner and trusting each other, and while each of them will stand, in a moment alone, each can do out of the group. This spiritual influence on the children is not only ten times that of one's own, but is ten times ten to the tenth. All the forces of the others are supporting him, and he is supporting all the others. That needs a group where there is trust in each other.

The deepest sorrow in the coming times will be when you trusted someone and he betrayed this trust. Broken trust will be the deepest sorrow for the people who are fighting for Michael in the coming times. Intuition is betrayed. One can't stand together any longer, but on one's own. When one has stood in such a group working together, one knows what a force is lost. One sees what a miserable being one is, and how little can be done standing alone.

But we can have courage to go into the next years. There will be a whirlpool of forces – in science, in social life, in education, in all fields. Luciferic and Ahrimanic forces will be there, but also forces of the good spirits working through them. If we wait for the secure knowledge that what we do is good, we won't move a finger. We have to handle situations out of Intuition. To withstand Ahriman and his forces, we will have to stand in a group of people who trust each other, help each other, and stand up for each other. Then the forces of good may work, but cannot so work when one of us is working alone.

This is what I would like to tell the younger people who are moving towards the 21st century. It is your time. It is your life. It is not a time when we older ones shall be active. Our generation was a generation of the middle of the century. Now we hand it over to you, the custodians of these forces in the next years.

As the outer forces work in a more chaotic way, even more than in the middle third of the century, I offer you the idea: 'Try to find groups, smaller or bigger, who work together not only to study, but to carry out responsible work in the world. Stand with each other so that those who are standing know they are not standing alone, that each is trusted, and that he can trust the others.'

The Good

The age of Atlantis has long slipped into the nearly unrecorded past and has, since Greek times and before, been to history nothing more than a mythical picture. It is a time of humanity washed away by water, by ice, by catastrophe, an epoch buried in the upheavals, the migrations, and transformations of evolution. Recorded history has erected its civilizations, its structures, its configurations upon the vanished time of this ancient age.

The face of the earth has changed. Land masses have shifted. Oceans have moved. The migrations of peoples, scattered in their different streams, still brought over, into the world after Atlantis, elements of the old wisdom and impulses for the new cultures. This world after Atlantis is called the post-Atlantean epoch, and we, living in the 20th century, have already moved into the fifth post-Atlantean period of this culture after Atlantis.

This fifth post-Atlantean period commences about A.D. 1500, a time that coincides approximately with the transition from the culture of the historical Middle Ages into the flowering of the Rennaissance. The early post-Atlantean periods recapitulated earth evolution until the Egyptian-Assyrian period, when the sentient soul became the vessel of spiritual development. This was the third post-Atlantean period and behind the story of man in this period evolutionary forces developed the sentient soul.

In this period of the sentient soul, mankind had the possibility of learning to internalize beauty. The sentient soul had the possibility in this time of mirroring beauty. This came about through the astral body which, confronted with the outer world, could act on it, while the outer world could act on the astral body. In this latter capacity, however, it was an organ of reaction to the world outside. The outer world had a direct action on the astral body, just as the astral body did on the world. With the development of the sentient soul, this process needed no longer be so direct. It could be experienced more as a mirror. The sentient soul could, so to speak, internalize the influence and beauty of the outer world. The outer world could then be relived as in an inner mind, in the sentient soul. In the sentient soul, then, could arise the feeling of beauty.

This period was followed by the Greco-Roman period, lasting into the Middle Ages. From internalized feeling the new experience entered into a discovery of internalized thought. This transference of thought *in* the world to thought *about* the world was possible through the awakening of a new soul capacity: the intellectual soul. The outer world could now be reflected in thoughts about it. These thoughts, hitherto perceived only as they were incorporated into the world itself, outside man, now came to be experienced as reflections about the world within man. They thus came to have a certain freedom from the world, in man, and he could experience them as happening within himself.

The highest ideal that man could aspire to in this new internalization of thought processes was that of truth. Truth, to the intellectual soul, became what beauty had been to the sentient soul – the apex of its development, the goal to be striven for. Just as striving to bring beauty to birth in the sentient soul had been the way of development in the early period, now the fight to arrive at inner truth became the path of development in the intellectual soul period.

This is strongly reflected in the development of Greco-Roman philosophy, but even more fiercely so in Christian times and in the Middle Ages when the search for truth also became the battle against error. The fight against error was like the sounding board of man's aspiration to truth. Truth was the millstone, in a certain sense, the grinding stone against which the intellectual soul had to be developed. Error was thought to be not just something wrong, but an impurity in the developing organ of the intellectual soul. Banishment, exile, and death were the penalties for error. The men of these times experienced the reality of this fight so strongly that they felt it better to burn men for error, and be burned for truth, than betray the cause. This is reflected in the great record of martyrs and heretics throughout these times.

As A.D. 1500 approaches, and Europe awakens to its languages and heritage, it sees for the first time outside itself the laws and orders of antiquity, and also begins to question dogma. A new faculty and new period begin to dawn. Observation and objectivity as methods begin to replace the scholastic arguments.

Science has, in the spirit of a new age, its first forerunners. They are no longer like the men of wisdom of old, repositories and revealers of the secrets, but a new cadre of discoverers. And the great humanists, in the same spirit, are observers of the scene of man and his history. All this heralds the period of the consciousness soul.

Whereas the intellectual soul had the task of avoiding error, the consciousness soul has the task of developing not truth, but the good, by encountering evil. The intellectual soul developed by internalizing truth; in the consciousness soul period, man has the task of evolving yet another soul by internalizing goodness.

For any man caught in the existential web of today's chaotic world of conflict, the question that arises out of his intellectual soul is: 'How do I develop this new consciousness faculty in order to find the good?'

This entails first of all the necessity of living in and with the world, for the Book of the Good, as it were, cannot be taken into a closet somewhere removed from men and read in the purity of the intellect.

Yet the modern man is caught in a tangle, because, to proceed on his search for the good, he must be able to build on a knowledge of the truth – and where, in the conflicting claims to truth rampant today, and in the denial of truth itself, can man secure this knowledge? The tangle goes deeper, for once caught in the sweeping actions of the world, how is the modern man who is encountering evil in a new spirit of consciousness to know whether in what he does he is doing the good? He may believe he is saying the truth, the truth gathered out of the intellectual past, but to speak truth even, is that the same as doing a good thing?

In the consciousness soul period we soon perceive that a thing can only enter the field of good when it is *done*. Goethe had already expressed this by saying, 'In the end, all things still must be done.'

Truth can be known; good can only be done.

And since the new mysteries of the age of consciousness are the mysteries, not of truth and error, but of the good, they are the mysteries of deeds: mysteries of the will.

The task of modern man is to encounter evil in order to create good. This is a transformation out of the passing era of the intellectual soul, when the task was to encounter error in order to create truth.

The study of anthroposophy in order to know things in a right way, in order to arrive at grasp of the truth, is only to take anthroposophy into the intellectual soul. To bring anthroposophy into the sphere of the consciousness soul 'all things have to be done'. It can not only be studied and known; it must be realized in the world.

Before speaking about how to find a way to realize the good, however, we must first understand the roots of evil.

Before the age of Atlantis, in the time of Lemuria, Lucifer came into the evolutionary field of mankind. This happened in the fifth period of Lemurian times when the Venus forces were leading men, and Lemurian culture had a development in the south, the region now covered by Malaya. Lucifer took his chance to get into Lemurian development and bring about a great change in the world – the change of sex: The division of mankind. With the presence of sexes, Lucifer could get a better hold of man. He could do this by bringing desires into the astral body of man.

The gift of this development was freedom.

The counterpart to this event comes in Atlantean times, in the culture of the Turanian people, when Ahriman could get a grip on the evolutionary field too. The Turanians turned the culture of the angel to the culture of the scorpion; they took the Toltec development of plant culture over, but converted sexual forces into magic powers with which they operated on the etheric world. Because of this, Ahriman could get his hold. He could do this by bringing error into the etheric body of man.

The gift of this development was self-consciousness.

In the period following Atlantean times, the Asuras take their opportunity to lay hold of the evolutionary field. These Asuras are dark Archai-beings. They seek to penetrate the ego. The ego is their field, just as the astral body was a field to Lucifer, and the etheric body to Ahriman. Their penetration can destroy the ego by snatching out parts of it, so to speak, and these stolen parts of the ego then take on a life of their own and act as demons. By doing this the Asuras bring to the physical body that element of the consciousness soul period: evil.

The gift of this development will be spiritual creativity.

We thus have a picture of how, in post-Atlantean times, the evolutionary thread is taken up and worked on by different forces. In the post-Atlantean development of the sentient and intellectual souls, we see first, a certain recapitulation of

Lemurian and Atlantean times. Just as Lucifer entered Lemurian times, so he worked into the sentient soul, bringing desires and passions. These desires and passions see the development of their counterparts in illness and death.

The good hierarchies gave us a help against these negative forces the forces of healing.

In the post-Atlantean development of the intellectual soul Ahriman enters, just as he entered Atlantean times. He works into the intellectual soul bringing the possibility of error. Ahriman thereby could have corrupted the whole of evolution, had not the good hierarchies given karma as a help against error. Individual karma is how error can be corrected in the life between death and rebirth. That is why during the period of the intellectual soul karma had to be not so much known, but rather experienced.

After A.D. 1500, the beginning of the consciousness soul period, the ego comes into its field of development. And it is in this period that the Asuras enter.

The Asuras infiltrate the ego. They seek to possess portions of the ego; these portions they detach from the ego proper, and out of these bits of stolen ego demons can be born. These demons, taking their life from the stolen ego-hood of man, became free to turn ego properties to their own purposes. Part of the egohood of man is thus turned into the stuff of demonic activity.

When this has happened, the results cannot be made good now in this period of earth development. Through the stolen ego portion of man the Asuras will be able to pursue their independent activity. Only in the future era of Jupiter development can these demons of human origin be reintegrated into the stream of earth's rightful evolution.

The Asuras work on the ego of man by bringing theoretical materialism into the life of man's consciousness soul, just as this consciousness soul is experiencing its evolutionary development. Grasping this theoretical materialism as a world outlook, people are cut off from a spiritual outlook and spiritual forces. The tendency then is to forget about real spiritual beings. The ego birth through the consciousness soul is aborted, and the victims of the Asuras turn often to a deep sensuality. Out of this they build grotesque hells of sensuality. These hells of sensuality tend to be caricatures of the earthly paradise, where material progress is cut off from its spiritual background and locked in a realm of sensual gratification.

The world view that accompanies this development is one of the human being as a bundle of purely material forces. Man, evolution, development, and culture are all looked at as a mere combination of the forces of chance. This view impersonalizes, despiritualizes, and fatalizes the whole picture of man's existence and essence. Steiner calls this kind of evil that emanates from the Asuras 'outpouring decomposition'.

There is an antidote in the material world to the Asuras. This is the practice of looking at the outer world as *an ocean of working willing forces*. Where the Asuras would capture the ego in the senses, the antidote is to look through the senses. The sensual web of life created by the increase in material well-being can be seen, not as an ocean of sensuality to drown in, but a vast show wherein will forces are seething, tumbling, swelling. But if one can look through the senses into this sea, seeing the forces not as mere sensations, but as waves and currents of will, then one can begin to grasp that these will forces are expressions of something still further behind the scene – the wisdom creating the world.

A modern man, however, now living in the birth pains of the consciousness soul, faces a world in which the Asuras are not only working but have already possessed extensive ego forces. How is one, in this situation, to go about developing forces for doing good? The Asuras, it was said, represent a force against development. In looking for an ego anchor in this situation, we must turn to the forces for development and grasp the concept of development itself which is suitable to the consciousness age. Anthroposophy can lead us to an understanding in this direction. It is in a sense an embodiment of a concept for development of the cosmos, of nature, and of man.

In 1500, at the beginning of the era of consciousness soul development, changes came about in the constitution of man. At about this time, in what Steiner describes as 'a cosmic thunderstorm', the First Hierarchy actually changed the possibilities of thinking in man. In olden times, all knowledge was knowledge of the heart. It permeated the thinking and will forces from the middle of man. From this middle, from the diaphragm, it irradiated every inner perception with warmth and enthusiasm.

About 1500, these living forces of thought 'shrivelled', so to speak. They shrank from the radiating middle of man to the brain only. Thought became cut off from the heart forces. This enabled man, through the medium of his brain, to become cool, objective, and intellectual in his thought life.

This transition time marks, and is marked by, the more or less simultaneous rise of modern science. This method of knowledge is rooted in a new standpoint for man. A standpoint of man as the onlooker. He is no longer the participator. Knowledge is derived from thought, removed to the brain, looking from a detached vantage point on the development of the cosmos and nature. The man is no longer himself engaged in the same way in the cosmos and nature that he now observes.

This has been the ascending and now reigning form of knowledge for more than 400 years. The great danger run by this science, which has been of immeasurable value to man, is the removal of man himself from the evolutionary development of earth. This phenomenon could be described in various ways – as an automaton world, or a world in which man grows gradually alienated from his spiritual connection. Religion fights an ever more difficult battle in trying to preserve such a connection.

It was out of this situation and predicament that Steiner moved, in the 1923 Christmas Foundation meeting, to give a basis for the new mysteries. He calls, in the Foundation Meditation, for men to exercise and practise spirit recollection, spirit mindfulness, and spirit vision. This is meant to be a new link to the spirit, suitable to the consciousness soul era, where the spiritual activity of the soul is to build out of practice in full awareness, so 'that good may become/what from our hearts we would found/and from our heads direct, with single purpose'.

What Steiner puts forth is a way of active inner development. This, in troubled times, is meant to be a way to reach a grasp of the good. But to become reality it must lead over into not just a good perceived, but a good that can be done.

A terrible dilemma in all doctrine is the rigid fixing of principles for all times. In our times, the chaos of moral values and assaults on the heritage of fixed principles reflects the transition from the intellectual soul era to the consciousness soul era. Truth was an aspiration to the absolute, which in a way was proper to the reachings of the intellectual soul. But when the intellectual soul tries to dictate from categories of truth the fixed principles of goodness, it fails. The intellectual soul at this moment confounds truth and the good. It over reaches itself and tries to possess the consciousness soul and transform it into intellectuality.

Where the intellectual soul properly tried to apprehend the eternal truth, as if forever stable in the fixed stars of a Ptolemaic cosmos, the consciousness soul seeks to penetrate into the good of a particular situation. In this sense the consciousness soul is existential, whereas the intellectual soul dealt with essences. Whereas truth, ideally, is absolute and everywhere, the good is never absolute. There is no good that is always and everywhere the good. The good is dependent on the situation only – the good is always a good in relation to something else.

To confound truth and good, to confuse the realms of the intellectual and consciousness souls, is to introduce endless strife and confusion into human affairs.

In this sense the new mysteries are not the mysteries of wisdom. Rather they are mysteries of the initiation of the will towards the good 'that may become'.

On the way towards seeking the good that may become, mankind has the good helpers out of the spiritual world.

The Archangel Michael, after the cosmic 'thunderstorm' of about 1500, saved his cosmic sun wisdom and brought it as Imaginations to the world after 1899. This was the time when the dark period of Kali-Yuga came to an end and spiritual light could again reach mankind.

Children, young people, men and women living in the 20th century could, by having gone through this cosmic school, have a deep remembrance in the unconscious part of the soul (the will) so that they might recognize spiritual wisdom wherever they would meet it on earth. Out of several springs, cosmic wisdom will come into the world in the 20th century and afterwards.

The Christmas foundation can be such a spring for people in the 20th century – but it is of the utmost importance to all, and sometimes to anthroposophists especially, to know that other springs will come to mankind too.

One of the spiritual circles around the Christ is the circle of what Indian wisdom called the Boddhisatvas. They are also helpers in the education of mankind – twelve helpers towards the good to become. Each 5,000 years one of the Boddhisatvas has to go down to earth to incarnate as a human being for many, many lives. In all these lives they bring into mankind – by their working – one of the twelve aspects of Christ.

The fourth one was known as Gautama Budda, who had his last incarnation, in fulfilling his task, around the year 600 B.C.

In this life as Gautama Buddha he could pull together all his forces to bring his task to earth again. This task was the learning of universal pity as a preparation for Christ's coming to mankind.

The next Boddhisatva to come is called by the Indians the Maitreya Boddhisatva. He has another task in the period of the consciousness soul development. As Steiner described it, he is to be 'the bringer of the good through the spoken word'.

In the period of the consciousness soul he is one of the greatest leaders of mankind, a helper of the good, which he brings through the power of the spoken word from mouth to ear. Steiner called him: 'He, who will set his words of good in the service of the Christ impulse in the etheric garment of the earth. He will speak words that develop magic moral forces in men. He will transfer moral will impulses to men by speaking words of the good.'

Since 1500 we have all been working out of thoughts that live in the head. Our hearts, too often, have been empty.

The new task is to fill our hearts with warmth for the spirit. We must warm our hearts for the real morality, for *doing* the good, so that this warmth may stream up to the head.

Through this the aim is to think and speak words of real consolation which can light real spiritual fire.

By speaking about anthroposophy in words that come from the heart and have gone through the clarification of the head we may stand in the helpful rays of him who serves the Christ through the spoken word.

Three Trials

Healing in the time of the consciousness soul opens a wide horizon. The healing of physical diseases and of mental diseases is to be done now, and it is a beautiful task, but healing means much more in the consciousness soul era – it means also healing in social life, in science, in education, and in the arts. Our age needs to be an age of hygienic impulses. If we want to be active in life in any field of healing, working on a spiritual basis, we must ask: 'Which spiritual being stands behind the good hygienic impulses of today?'

Instead of speaking abstractly, we have to ask the question, 'Who is the being, the real being, in and behind an undertaking?' To answer the question of which spiritual being is behind healing, I will tell a tale from the Old Testament. St. John the Evangelist wrote the Apocalypse, giving insight into the future of mankind; but in the Old Testament there is also a little Apocalypse – the story of Tobias.

Rembrandt was much inspired by the story of Tobias; in hundreds of drawings and paintings and even etchings, he turned to that story – the story of Tobias and the fish. It took place in Babylon, during the exile of the Jewish people under King Nebuchadnezzar and his son. But though the story takes place in an historical period, it is not so much an historical happening as, rather, a preview. If we ask what future it is written for, I would say for our time now. The tale of Tobias is the story of mankind in the problems of our time.

In Babylon old Tobias lived, and he was blind. He was called old Tobias the Righteous. He was always right. He held the right rituals, and he carried out the law exactly. He was one of those responsible for upholding the laws of the Jewish people in a time of exile. This was risky. For example, he buried the dead according to the Jewish laws, though it was forbidden. He risked his own life.

Once, when he had buried one of his friends in the right way (at night because he couldn't do it in the day without being put in prison), he sat down in the early morning, tired, and looked up to heaven. He gave thanks. A swallow flew over. Its hot dung fell in his eyes. He was blinded. Old Tobias, the man who was always right, goes blind – but he does not rebel.

Old Tobias lived with his wife, Anna, a little dog, and his son, young Tobias. The family pulled together, but old Tobias, who was once rich, and who helped many friends, is now blind. He can't work. He spent his money and grew poor.

One day he said to his son, young Tobias: 'You must go to my friend Gabelus far away, in the land of the Medes.' This meant the boy would have to cross the deserts and the river Tigris. 'You must go into the land of Gabelus and ask him for the silver I once lent him when he was in difficulty. I need it now.'

This story is full of symbols. For example, old Tobias once lent silver to Gabelus and now wants the silver back. Silver is always related to the moon, to the old wisdom. Old Tobias had once given away his wisdom, his old wisdom. Now he was blind. He wanted back the wisdom.

Old Tobias said: 'You can't make this journey alone. You must find a friend. This friend will be your companion. Go. Find a friend.'

Young Tobias went to the market and looked. In the marketplace he met a very fine young man who looked at him with friendly, radiant eyes. Soon they were friends. Young Tobias asked him if he would be his companion on the journey to the land of the Medes, where his father's friend Gabelus lived, and the new friend agreed.

Young Tobias brought his companion to the old father who said to the stranger: 'Though I can't see you, your voice gives me confidence.' This is a sign of Inspiration. Old Tobias couldn't see the outer world, but he could feel confidence through Inspiration. The pair were given gifts for their journey and they set out together with the little dog.

Going on a journey means following a way of inner development. Young Tobias was going 'on the way' – he was going the way of inner development. This was such a path, not just an outer journey through the deserts and over a river.

From the beginning the companion, though he appeared to be a young man, revealed himself as a teacher. During the journey through the desert, the friend of young Tobias was at the same time his teacher.

They reached the river Tigris. It was already evening. His guide told young Tobias to go into the water and catch a big fish. Tobias went into the water, and a very big fish swam up. Tobias was very much afraid. His companion on the bank said: 'Don't be afraid. Catch the fish with both your hands, and pull him on to the land.'

So they pulled the big fish on to the land, and the friend and Tobias took out the gall bladder and the liver and the heart, and they put the gall bladder into one basket, and the liver and the heart into another one. Then the companion said: 'Now you have stood your trial. You can go on – you will have the forces to heal your father and to help your cousin Sarah.'

Young Tobias was astonished that he was to help his cousin Sarah, because he knew her strange story. This cousin, the daughter of the brother of his father, lived in another town. They had to go through this town on the way to the Medes. When they entered, they went to his uncle, who said: 'Though I have never seen you before you bear such a great resemblance to my brother Tobias that I see at once you must be his son. Who is your friend?'

'My companion on the journey,' Tobias answered.

'Well, come in, you two, and be my guests,' cried the uncle.

Then the companion said: 'We shall not only be your guests, but young Tobias is chosen by God to be the husband of Sarah.'

At this the uncle was very shaken. He said: 'Oh no, don't let it be.'

Now what about Sarah? She was a beautiful, but a very unhappy girl. Because of her beauty, many young men wanted to marry her. Seven bridegrooms in turn had come, but each time she married, in the night when the young man went to touch her, he dropped dead. Seven young men met this end. The uncle said: 'The shame of my family shall be increased no more. Young Tobias will not be the eighth.'

Tobias insisted. He was brought to Sarah, who told him to avoid her because she was possessed by a bad demon (the demon was called Asmodeus).

But the marriage took place. Afterwards they went to the marriage chamber. Before Tobias touched her, however, he knelt down and took the liver and the heart of the fish, as his companion had bade, and laid them on the fire and burned them. The demon departed out of Sarah and flew into the desert. Sarah was free.

The companion had gone, meanwhile, to the land of the Medes and fetched the silver. The journey home began.

More than a year had passed, and old Tobias for the first time in his life was rebellious. He was rebellious now because, he said, 'I have always done the right things, I have always practised the right rituals. God sent me blindness and I did not rebel. But now I have sent away my son Tobias and he does not return. God has taken my son from me.' In the moment that old Tobias rebels, the little dog trots in the door. The mother rushes out and sees the others approaching. She is astonished to see a young woman with them.

When they come in, young Tobias goes to his father. He now has the second task; to heal his father. He takes the gall out of the bladder and puts it on the eyes of his father. Old Tobias sees again and praises God.

In that moment, the companion reveals himself. He stands there in his true radiance, and he says: 'I am the Archangel Raphael, one of the seven angels standing around the throne of God.' Thus does Raphael reveal himself as the healing angel. As they start to thank him, he vanishes. They fall on their knees and give thanks to God.

Who is Raphael? Throughout the Middle Ages, Raphael was viewed as the helper of the sick. According to the beliefs of the Middle Ages, Raphael had to do with the forces of the depths – the forces of the depths in man. We call these forces desires, which come up from the depths into conscious life. To bring the forces of darkness out of the depths of earth and of man – to bring it to the healing light of Christ – that was the work of Raphael.

He is often represented with the staff of Mercury in hand. In pre-Christian times the staff of Mercury had two snakes climbing around it – symbols at once of evil, and of spirit. Raphael, however, is shown, not with two snakes, but with two rising flames. A staff bearing two flames. In the flame evil is burned and brought again into evolution and development.

In medieval descriptions of Raphael, 'Raphael is one of the four faces of Christ'. One was Christ Triumphant – shown in the face of Michael. Christ, the Judge, was Uriel. Christ, the Initiator, was Gabriel. Raphael was Christ the healer.

People in the Middle Ages knew that, when speaking of Christ, there were these several facets, several possibilities for reaching Him. One, the healing side, was the face of Raphael.

In the twentieth century, in the culture of our time, we still call upon Raphael the healing force, one of the seven angels standing around the throne of God.

In the Apocalypse, we are told about the beast coming out of the waters. This means the forces of the depths, which are coming to the surface and are visible now, all around us. Man has gone over a threshold of the merely visible world. Though he doesn't know it, he is looking into the forces which are behind the merely visible world. Those forces are coming to the surface and are showing through what is going on now. Man must be prepared to encounter these forces and not to be afraid. That is a great thing to learn now, to look at those forces of the depths, but not be afraid. For the modern task is to change them. It is a task of bringing them back into development and into a right course of evolution again.

What are these forces?

The first of these forces, coming from the depths of human life, are the forces of sexuality. They are everywhere you look, especially in the western world.

I was in Berlin about 1949, shortly after the war. When you use the subway, if you do not have a map of Berlin, you do not know whether you will get out in the East or the West sector. One station is in the West sector, the next in the East, and perhaps the next again in the West. The subway was not built on today's borderline, but on an older conception of Berlin. So you had to be careful that you didn't get out in East Berlin if you didn't want to, and weren't prepared. However, it was very easy to know if you were in the West or the East. When you looked out of the window and saw some advertising with a half-naked lady, you were in the West sector. In the East sector you found only pictures of ugly men.

In the middle of Lemurian times, Lucifer divided the sexes, making man and woman. An impulse stirred them to seek each other and be united again. Was this only to wrong man? No, Lucifer was a helper of evolution, because the great task of our planet is to develop from the old planet of wisdom into the future planet of love. Love is the objective of the whole Earth. In the school of love, man had to learn the first steps. Sexual love, which, as such is Luciferic, is a first step in this school.

The next step is family love, love between parents and children. Gabriel taught it to mankind. The third step is to love the ego of another person – to recognize another person as an ego. It makes no difference whether it is a man or woman. It is an ego. This step is taught by Michael.

The last step is love of mankind. This is taught by Christ himself.

Sexual love, as the first step, develops to the second step, family love. We learned this in the times before Christ. Nowadays, we have to learn to love the ego of another. In the future we have to learn love for mankind. It is easy to say we love mankind, but it is very difficult to do. We still have to wait to understand love for mankind. Once we have attained to love of mankind, Lucifer will be free from his task. Man will have freed Lucifer.

Lucifer divided man and woman, placing in the astral body the impulse of sexual love. Lucifer provides resistance; our powers may grow against this resistance. In the present, sex enters culture in a brutal way. With our fathers and grandfathers this force was hidden behind the curtains. Now it is coming into the open in a brutal way. We have to hold out against it. We have to learn to deal with these things without being overabsorbed in them. We learn to look and say, 'Yes, that is something that exists in the world. It is a fact of life. And why not?'

But the ego should not be disturbed by it. Encountering these forces, we must know that they were put in the astral body. They are there for good reasons, as a first step to love. In the next step we learn to enter family love, which is somewhat more serene. During life, we may even try to find real love for the ego of another. This is a great step. That is all that one can do now. One may have just an inkling of what the fourth stage of love could be, in the future life of mankind. When developing those forces of sexuality into forces of love for mankind, the companion on the journey is the Archangel Raphael.

However, a second type of force lies in the depths, and is now coming up. In Lemurian times, men and women were divided. At the beginning of Atlantean times, man and world were divided. The picture for this is man thrown out of Paradise. In the state of Paradise, man was one with the world, and the world was one with him. In Atlantean times came a division of man and the world, and, with it, the possibility for Ahriman to bring in error.

A large group of people in Atlantean and post-Atlantean times took on a specific task: to incarnate for work on the face of the earth. They called themselves the sons of Cain. The sons of Cain dealt with the surface of the earth with their hands, creating a man-made landscape. If you travel much about the world, you can see the difference between man-shaped landscapes and wild landscapes. For example, in Europe, whole regions have been formed and shaped by man. In the Scandinavian lands, whole regions are untouched by human hands; they are wild, empty, and half-demonic.

The sons of Cain were the first ones to build houses, to promote architecture, to work on the earth, to humanize nature, and to improve earth so that it might be man-made in the good sense.

This impulse came under the influence of Ahrimanic errors. Ahriman said: 'Yes, you must improve the earth. Don't be content with what the earth has brought you. You should build a new technical man-made world.'

We are on our way to building that technical man-made world. When you come into New York, you see a world which is not a humanized landscape, but a wholly man-made world. There is nothing natural left in it.

What error has Ahriman injected in man? The lust for power over the earth – the lust for possession. Power and possession belong to the second force which has come out of the depths of human beings. Ahriman tries to bring this lust for power and possession so that man may build up a technical world, not what the Hierarchies want for mankind's evolution. The will to possess all things demonizes man. After the last war in Europe, when Holland had had a year of starvation, you could see this at work: the first thing after the war was, 'We want to eat. We want to have eating.' Houses were full of things to eat. Finally people were satisfied. Then came the next step. They wanted clothes. There was a great wave of clothes buying. Everyone bought and bought, even if he had already two or three or five of a thing. He bought more because he wanted to possess clothing. But we couldn't have more possessions than we had room for in our house, so the next thing was housing – going into real estate. Yes, possessing a piece of earth, and the house upon it. Then cars. In Europe the streets are so full that you can go better on foot, and be there sooner than in your own car. These gorging forces come up from the depths. Ahriman will not be freed from bringing the lust for power and possessions until we have attained an unselfish relation to the world.

Just as we have to transform the Luciferic sexual forces, by stages, into love for the spiritual ego of another, correspondingly, we have to find an unselfish relation to the world. The Rosicrucians of the Middle Ages knew this well, and they had a proverb: 'The eye shall not desire, but the eye shall love.'

Think about what marketing is doing today. Marketing tries to put desire in the eyes, through packaging. What is a modern car except an object of desire, only secondarily for transportation. The forces in our culture are brutal in trying to force one into desire: in advertising, on TV, radio, in magazines, papers, billboards and signs, it is all trying to infect us with the desire to buy, the desire to possess. It is very difficult not to desire a thing of beauty, but just to love it for its beauty.

A third force out of the depths is that of destruction. Our living body is a body of building things up, but it is also a body which is continually destroying. It destroys old cells to build new cells. Our blood lives for only three or four weeks. Then we have renewed it totally. This means that all the time life is destroyed to build up new life. These forces of destruction are forces in our metabolism. We take in food and destroy it totally. We do not only split up molecules of albumen, but reduce them to their smallest particles. Steiner reports how this splitting force goes much further, to the extent that substance is driven into chaos again.

In our metabolic system substance disappears. As it disappears in our metabolism, a stream of etheric forces flows in through the senses, through eyes and ears. They stream into the body and are built up into new substance. This is the great mystery of our metabolic system. Our bodies are not built out of the food we eat. Rather we eat food so that we can destroy it. When the substance is destroyed, there arises a vacuum. Into this vacuum, through our senses, we bring in new etheric forces. The substance of the human body is young new substance which wasn't in the world before. In this way, Steiner says, human beings renew matter – but we are not conscious of it.

Here the Asuras enter. The Asuras teach us how to destroy atoms. With the knowledge of how to destroy atoms, they teach us also how to destroy the world. We have learned consciously to destroy. But we have not learned *consciously* to build up new young living substance which can receive into itself the creative spirit. True, in a technical way we rearrange atoms and molecules to make new molecules; in the future we may even make molecules which have the appearance of living material. But in laboratory, factory, or shop we cannot build up new, young, living substance that can receive creative spirit.

We shall have to learn this in the future. Meanwhile, the Asuras work with forces of fear – fear of total annihilation, fear of the black empty nothing. When the atom bomb came it brought an explosion of fear in the world. Now that we are a little bit acquainted with atom forces, we tell ourselves that the great explosion won't happen. The atomic forces are safely stored away, we say; they are there for our convenience, not to destroy the world. But still, deep in man, there is this fear. If you speak with many young people in Europe now, there is deep down in their feeling a mood of fear on the one side, and of hopelessness on the other. 'What shall I do? Why should I try to develop myself? One atom bomb, and poof!'

This the Asuras want – that we feel fear. The Asuras are spirits of anti-development. Raphael, instead, is the spirit of the journey of inner development. Going 'on the way' – that is where Raphael helps.

Lucifer wants the old to continue. Lucifer is a real conservative. Ahriman wants to use the old for his own egotistic purposes. The Asuras want the old to be annihilated.

We can only fight and free the Asuras when we are able to develop a love for development itself. This is the very being of Raphael, the love of development. Love of mankind, love of the outer world, love of the earth, of our higher being, of culture – love of what can be in the future. And in all these, love for development as such.

There are steps in the school of love in this field too. There are ways of learning how to love that which develops in the future. When you look at a young child, you can learn to feel more than just family love, or love of all that is young and dear. You can look at such a young child and say, 'Out of this child much can develop. I don't know what it will be, but I love what is there, which has not yet been developed, but shall develop in the future.'

It is one of the great gifts of the gods, when they allow you to be a grandfather. With your own child you have to deal with family love, and you are a little bit blind. From your grandchildren you have more distance. You can see them better. You can try to learn to love their development.

In this sense for development lies the true renewal of the schools, the renewal of education. The spirit of Waldorf School

Education should be the love of what will develop in the future. This means to help young beings to develop their forces in their own ways – not as we think best. Our task is not to impose our views upon the development of another person. We should hold ourselves back, and just love what is developing towards the future. That is one of the first steps on the way towards the love of development itself.

The same is true for people who are really living with plants, in agriculture. Look at the real farmer, who walks around over the fields, and looks at them, and sees the sprouts coming up. He has a feeling, love perhaps, for what is coming. So it may be in art and in science – we can learn to love, not only what is, but what is to be.

When we try to build up a picture of modern man, we can say: 'Here he stands. Over him is Michael, the great spirit of the sun, bringing spiritual thinking, giving men the forces for action out of spiritual thinking. Beneath and a little behind him is Raphael, the spirit of Mercury, transforming sexual love into love of mankind, the need for power and possession into love for the world, the will to destroy into a love for development.'

Seen from one side, these are the three trials of modern man.

From the other side, these three trials call forth three healing impulses of Raphael.

If man stands between Michael, who brings him spiritual thinking and strength for action, and Raphael, bringing him the love for development, then mankind can meet the Christ on the way into the future.

The New Morale

On Golgotha, the physical crucifixion of Christ was a fact; this crucifixion brought renewal to the dying earth. Nature received a surplus of life forces again. Mankind also received new forces in his physical constitution. Christianity since Golgotha is a history of a first attempt by mankind to perceive the glory of Christ. It is only a first attempt.

Steiner tells us that Christ, now as a spiritual being, was crucified again by the materialism of the 19th century. This 19th-century crucifixion was not a physical one, but a crucifixion in the etheric world of the human thinking. Out of this etheric crucifixion there was an etheric resurrection. Since the year 1933, the end of the first third of the 20th century, Christ has reentered the etheric world for mankind – this etheric world where man lives in thinking, imagination, and images. When mankind seeks Christ now, wanting to have a real meeting with the spiritual being, he has to seek Christ in this etheric world.

Friedrich Schiller, 150 years ago, in his letters on *The Aesthetic Education of Man*, tells us that man lives between the forces of form and matter. Between forces of form and forces of matter is what he calls the realm of the 'play instinct'. The word 'impulse' is better. The real artist is the one who is able to play in the highest sense, just as a little child plays. He gives to matter a higher being by playing with it. The real artist, working out of this impulse, lives between form and matter. In form he gives expression to laws of the spiritual world; in matter he gives expression to how matter wants to be expressed. With marble, he can make something which is more than marble – it becomes an idea in marble.

Ideas which are visible in matter when the artist handles it come from a world of play – play with reality.

Schiller said that the greatest artist is the educational and social artist; he is the one who works with the most precious material: man. In the *art* of education, in the *art* of social life, we live in a world of 'the middle forces'. This is a world of rhythmical work, also dealing on one side with matter, and on the other side with spiritual forms or laws. Living in the reality of this middle region, we are in the same world where the resurrection of the etheric Christ is a reality.

Steiner said in lectures of 1911–1912 that, after 1933, there would be a reappearance of a new working of Christ in the etheric world of this 'middle region'. In one lecture he gives us three conditions which man has to fulfil, so that he may enter this world where the living etheric Christ is working.

The first condition, Steiner says, is that we have to have a feeling of the worthlessness of outer human existence. It's very simple. We all say, of course, that we have it. Do we have it? Do we really have a deep feeling of the worthlessness of outer human existence? Or are we hanging on to this outer human existence very much; very much more than we think, perhaps?

The second condition is the feeling of being unsatisfied with the materialistic explanations given in our culture of today – words that are 'stones for bread'. Perhaps we are a little bit unsatisfied with it. But when we are reading our newspaper each day, again and again, we are in this world where people are highly satisfied with the explanations given in this materialistic world.

The third condition is the feeling of inner duality, of inner split I may say, between that which I can do, and that which I ought to do. This feeling is as if on earth I were a dwarf, while my spiritual being – my cosmic being – were immense. With this feeling we come to the inner question – a question we have to ask ourselves not only between lunchtime and dinner, but for years and years – about our inadequacy and duality. It is a split between what we are on earth here, and what our higher egos ask us to do. Out of such a deep experience of insufficiency, Steiner says, the new morale of our age will arise.

The new morale is the morale of universal pity – compassion with all that suffers. No one, he said, who has knowledge about the spiritual reality of the world should be able to sleep at night so long as there is suffering in the world. Hopefully we sleep a little bit each night, but should we? When we really seek for the meeting with the etheric Christ, we will go through the same sufferings He went through – the crucifixion of materialistic thinking from the 19th century on.

When we want to prepare to meet the etheric Christ, when our karma is so far developed that we are able to have this meeting, then we shall have to go through these trials. They are existential trials. Out of modern existentialism these ordeals are coming into our existence. They cannot be avoided. Steiner says, when people go through these trials, Christ will speak out of the grey depths of the spirit. Out of the grey depths of the human spirit, He will speak words of consolation. But He will speak those words of consolation only for those who have really suffered existential pain and distress about the suffering of the world.

We want our ease. We want our security. But he who wants to meet the reality of the world – and the reality of the world is the reality of the resurrection of Christ in the etheric world – he has to live with uneasiness and with insecurity. This is our lot in social life. Steiner says Christ will only be met on the boundary of the bearable, in the shattered soul. Then He will give consolation, by giving insight into the laws of evolution. The great consolation which Christ will give is insight into the laws of evolution.

This can be the background of social work. If you want to go into social work, if you want to go into education, if you want to go into work with displaced, maladjusted, and delinquent persons, or into medical or industrial rehabilitation, this Christ insight can be the background of your work. Social work can only be done when we leave behind all missionary haughtiness and arrogance. We must leave behind all talking down to people. In one's heart, one will see how much talking down to people one is doing. We know the right answers. But they are not our answers; we got them from Rudolf Steiner. With those answers, we often speak down to people. Anthroposophists, I include myself, should have some modesty in telling other people about social issues. Have we been able to give a good example? We know the right ways, but we act as sectarians when we bring them only as knowledge.

Dr. Zeylmans once gave a lecture in Holland. He spoke about anthroposophy and said that it ought not to be sectarian. A lady asked: 'Dr. Zeylmans, tell me, what is a sect?'

He answered: 'A sectarian is one who gives answers to questions that have not been asked.'

Social work is full of pitfalls. Always you are tempted to give prefabricated answers. But don't pull these answers out! They are unsatisfying. When going into a social situation to work together with other people it is better to go with the feeling: I shall not be able really to answer the question put to me. On the other side, one should be ready to seek, together with the other persons, for the answers. That means we have to enter into the life of the other one and share with him his search for the answer. Real social life, social help, is to help the other to find the next step in his own evolution.

When someone asks me: what is the consciousness soul? I can be a good anthroposophical scholar and give the right anthroposophical answers. But living in the consciousness soul means the courage of meeting doubt, hatred, and fear. It means to be ready to meet doubt – about what you know, what you are, and what you do. It also means being ready to deal with the hate in the world against the spirit. You meet this as a doctor with officials who must approve new medicines. A wave of hate lives in the room while discussing these problems. We have to deal with it. It is the reality of the consciousness soul time. We have to take risks, because doing something out of the spirit is a very risky thing. One never knows where it will go. In the end, it means meeting evil.

We can learn from modern scientists. Modern science, in the upper echelons, has positive doubts about the reality of its concepts and its hypothesis – at least a top scientist will. Again and again, he tests his hypotheses, knowing they are only hypotheses as far as the observation of things go up till now. Even if these hypotheses are materialistic ones, the scientist doubts as a way of inner development. We can learn this from modern science, learn to live with insecurity and doubt.

Modern professional life also teaches ways to work together. When we have a job anywhere, we have to work with all kinds of people. This also is a way of inner development which modern life teaches us. Young people who are coming into anthroposophy should have a couple of years in modern professional life to learn to live together working with all kinds of people.

Think about the modern industrial leaders. They must take risks. They must develop courage. They must learn to live with insecurity. They have tremendous responsibility. When we look at people of about forty, directors of big firms, we can ask where they find the inner courage, the inner security to live with the risks they have to take. What forces do they live from? It's a big question, but I can perhaps suggest that they have these forces out of initiations in older cultures. The old initiates, where are they? In industry. Their initiation has gone down to their will. Out of this wisdom of their will, and the strength of their will, they can bear the insecurity and the great risks of modern professional life. This life in their wills, however, doesn't come up to their heads.

To help them means to bring that which is already living in their will up to their heads, so that it may become conscious. We don't have to teach them anything new. They already know. But they know in their will. We only have to awaken their wills into consciousness. This is where we can help.

In social life, we can try to find a way of developing consciousness soul concepts, but not with our stereotyped anthroposophical answers. An answer out of the real situation alone counts. That means entering into the life of the other one. It is not our task to quote Steiner or anyone whom the other does not know. That is taking away part of the other's freedom. The real task is to bring sensible, reasonable social concepts according to the situation at hand, not according to our predilections of foreknowledge.

In the beginning of the 1920s, Steiner once sat together with a group of friends who were responsible for the Threefold Commonwealth in that time. He spoke the following words, which were written down: 'You don't think, my friends, that if the Threefold Commonwealth were to be accepted in Württemberg (it was the time about 1921 when it was a question whether the Threefold Commonwealth would be accepted in Württemberg) that each mayor and each minister of state should be an anthroposophist, do you?' he asked. But they all thought it.

We have the task to bring reasonable, sensible social concepts, and they will find their own ways, their own development. Our task is to bring these concepts free, to give them away into life. They will find their own ways of development. That means living with the freedom of other people. He who lives out of anthroposophy in social life has to live in such a tension.

We have the world of ideas which we learn by studying anthroposophy. We also have the world of social reality. The great problem is how these two shall meet. Just as East is East and West is West, and never the twain shall meet, so ideas are ideas and social realities are social realities, and never may they meet. But a middle ground between them is the one of what I call sensible social concepts.

People in the world of social reality live in a tension between the reality they are standing in and the sensible social concepts they are looking for. We, as anthroposophists, live in a double tension, between ideas which are high and everlasting on the one side, and a translation of these ideas, which have eternity in them, into sensible social concepts which we can bring to the world. We can only develop sensible social concepts when we know social reality. This is like the middle ground between matter and form which Schiller speaks about.

About four times a year, I lead a management course for top executives. This means that twelve to fifteen directors of big firms, only the top ones, come together for a week. This is not an easy week. I come together with them, my knees shaking, and I ask myself: who am I to talk to these big bosses, each with immense responsibility, immense capital, immense numbers of people behind them? I know if I make a mistake speaking only about beautiful ideas I shall fail because those people cannot connect beautiful ideas with the social reality they stand in. I could speak about Saturn, and Sun, and Moon development, and I could speak to them about the future, the Threefold Commonwealth and a world as it should be. This would not help them.

We have to create an inbetween world. We have to come down from ideas so that they can come up from the social reality. Then they can say: 'We are speaking with someone who knows our social reality on the one side and can bring us social concepts which can help us to solve our problems.'

What are these sensible social ideas? Remember that we can only help these people when we are speaking out of 'middle forces'. That is the world of rhythm, the world of development. The first thing to clarify is the difference between growth and development. They are coping with problems of growth. Their firms are expanding. They show us the curves hanging on the wall behind the table. The big boss always has something like that behind his desk. 'This is the growth of my firm in the last ten years,' he says.

Now what is this growth? Is it a reality or not? Yes, it is a kind of reality. It is the reality of the quantitative aspect of the world. The boss says: 'This is the growth of capital investment; this is the growth of the people working in the firm; this is the growth of the products we are producing.' It seems as if growth is a continuing thing.

The other part of reality is the reality of development. Development is not a continuous thing. Development is something which is non-continuous. There was a typical poineer firm with one man who founded it at the top, and the whole organization going down from him. Then came the moment when the firm grew so big that he could not do everything himself. He could not have all things in his hands, and he had to differentiate the work. He could not be the only boss. He had to take two others, one for financing and marketing, the other for production. He himself kept up the research. The time for dividing the work came. Differentiation brings about change in the whole inner style of working. There is often a big crisis when a pioneer firm has to go over to this second stage of organization. If this is done right, growth can begin anew. If it is not done right, the firm will fail or be bought out after a couple of years.

Perhaps a firm becomes very prosperous. Here again comes a certain borderline of possibilities. The firm has now expanded to thousands of employees. They are all directed from a central board of directors. They are all in special departments with special tasks. There are advisory boards, line functions, and so on, but communication grows ever more difficult. Unless something is done, and a new kind of organization formed, things will not go on. This is the problem of most bigger firms. They have what they call scientific management with differentiation. But then they have to go on to integration of human possibilities and human objectives, so that human beings may develop in their work on the one side, while the objectives of the firm can be reached also. This creates the new work of today which is integration of the human and the technical factor.

This requires a quite new concept of management, of co-operating, of leadership. The question even arises: how big can a group be and work together effectively? Often a firm of 5,000 men has to be split up into subdivisions, each with their own life and direction, their own tasks and objectives. Individual objectives are set for the smaller unit.

Now we say: a graph like this shows the path of growth; the time has come to look at it in another way. There were the ways of working during the time of the pioneer period. Here is another period coming, for ten to fifteen years perhaps, of realizing scientific management. This development is quite another thing from growing. Growing is a continuity. It is only quantitative. When speaking about development, qualitative problems arise. We have to look at the quality – of organization, of leadership, of production, of personnel, and so forth.

After this introduction, the company leaders need a long

discussion on their own. They must integrate the light of these sensible social concepts of development with their own social reality. They have to ask themselves: where do we stand? Are we at the end of our pioneer period? This starts clarification. But what is going on?

The laws of evolution, the laws of rhythmical life, the laws of 'the middle' are penetrating the reality of social life.

The laws of biography in human life also enter the discussion. With human life, we can make a graph. We can take the first twenty-one years and show an overflow of living forces. Then there are twenty-one years during which the building up and running down of the physical forces are in equilibrium. After the beginning of the forties, we are all running down, whether we want it so or not. We see that we have to use spectacles to read. The physical body begins to stiffen. This is a physical reality. Each of us has to find a way of living with this reality. We go on and ask: is psychological development just the same? Look here: in the chart, we have an upcurve, and then comes the moment where there is a moment of freedom to choose the way of going down. Shall we go along with our physical capacities, or find quite a new level of spiritual psychological functioning? If we identify ourselves, our feeling of self-security, with physical things, with physical abilities, our productivity will go down with the physical let-down. If we are able to separate our feeling of self-security from our physical ability to do everything ourselves, then we shall be free, and we will see how to come, at the end of our forties and in our fifties, to a new level of spiritual activity which is quite a different one from the one between the twenty-first and forty-second years.

It is necessary also to speak about special fields, like marketing and to say that in marketing there are also such levels of possibilities. There is the level of marketing in the pioneer phase, having to do with clients who are known personally. One has a personal feeling and a personal knowledge of the people using the products.

In the second phase, contact is lost. There are too many. In a larger market the people are unknown, leading to the necessity of market research. This makes for uneasiness, but what other way is there?

Then comes a new concept of marketing, which works co-operatively between product and consumer. Knowing the real needs of the consumer requires discussion with him. There will no longer be price competition, but service competition. Service competition means to research the needs of the consumer, and help him solve his problems, not mine. How can I, as a producer, help to solve the problems of the consumer? It is the same as saying: I must go to the other party and give answers to the questions he has, not to the questions I have.

These are the kinds of questions we deal with in our conferences for the Management Association in Holland. Afterwards, participants say: 'We thought when we came that we would get some new gimmicks and new techniques. We got quite another thing. We didn't get one new technique, we didn't get one new gimmick, but we did get new horizons, and we are now thinking about our own working in quite another way.'

Such a response means that we have helped people in their evolution. It is no help to them to say: 'Steiner has said money should disappear in thirty years.' It is true, but what help is it to say it in this way?

Many participants in these conferences go home very happy to have received new social concepts, sensible new social ideas, with which they can take a long view of the problems of development they are in. There are others, usually very few, who come afterwards and say: 'Now tell me, you must have more behind this than you have told us.'

I answer: 'Yes, I have a world of ideas from which I translate problems into the language of sensible social concepts. When you become interested in this world of ideas, we can speak about it together. Of course, you are free, just to take the sensible social concepts, and they will do their work.'

About 4,500 people from top levels have gone through such courses in the last seven to eight years. That means that when you go into a factory in Holland, there is some knowledge about this. I can't say they all use it, but they do know about it and this creates an atmosphere in which next steps can be taken in the next thirty years.

The world is full of questions. The only question for us is: are we able to give helpful answers? Are we able to translate the world of eternal ideas into a world of sensible social concepts as Steiner taught them, and taught us to find them? Are we able to leave others free to do with the social concepts what, according to their possibilities, they want to do with them? And when they don't want to do anything with them, leave them free not to do anything?

About eight years after one of the directors of one of our big aeroplane factories in Holland participated in such a conference, I got a telephone call from his colleague: 'My co-director is resigning next week,' said the man, 'so I can go on now with the work we began eight years ago. I had to wait, because he couldn't grasp it, and I had to work together with him. Now he has resigned, and I am ready to take the first step. Please come in and have a talk with us about what should be the next step.' The next step was that the whole top level of this concern should come for a few days to a hotel and talk over what next steps might be taken. But I am not able to tell them what they have to do. I have not the knowledge of the social reality of their firm. They have it. But when we come together, they bring their social reality, and I, perhaps, help them with some sensible social concepts.

One of the problems of social life is the problem of payment. Steiner once said an astonishing thing: 'The concept of karma and reincarnation will have no chance to penetrate into social life, so long as people are paid as they are now.' We have to think this over. We have to find answers about the manner of payment. When everything as we know it now ends, and we have a Threefold Commonwealth in the world – a co-operative economic life, an equal political life, and a free spiritual life – then this might no longer be a question. But that ideal may only arrive perhaps in 3,000 to 4,000 years.

At present, we have to help people understand not the end of step sixty-one, but the next step. What has to be done now. We have to find the next steps in the problems of payment. This is a problem today – the problem of a fair wage or equitable payment. What is equitable payment? What is a fair wage? It is an important spiritual problem.

Nowadays, man is paid according to the amount, or the quality, of the work done. This is also true for the director. The man on the shop floor is paid for the quantity, the amount of work done, while the higher people are paid for the quality of work done. But, in both cases, for work done. On the shop floor, we have the piece-rate payment. The world wishes to get rid of it. I don't know how it is at this moment in the United States, but in Europe both management and labour want to get rid of piece-rate payment and to have people on fixed salaries. In the sixties, practically the whole metal and machine industry of Holland changed over to fixed monthly payments for all people. Production did not go down at all. There were people who said: 'When you do that, production will go down.' It didn't go down – on the contrary.

Now, is this already a solution? No. Perhaps it is one little step in the way we want to go. But how can we understand that the ideas of karma and reincarnation cannot come into the world as long as people are paid as they are?

By paying for work done, people are the slaves of their abilities. You are paid for your abilities, but your abilities are your old karma. It should be self-evident that I give my old karma, in the form of work, to the world, It should be self-evident that I give the possibilities I have, my capacities, as work to the world, as a gift to the world.

But people should have payment so that they may have the *possibility to develop new abilities and new concepts for the future.*

This would be payment not for what I can do, but for what I shall do – for developing new abilities and new concepts. That takes time.

One new concept in the field of sensible social concepts means, for a normal man, about two, three, four, or five years of work. When, in three or four years, you have one good idea, you can be very happy. But people must live at the same time.

We give old karma back to the world; this is self-evident. But we have to live to be able to get new ideas and develop new concepts. The question is: how can we develop and realize sensible social concepts while still meeting the obligations of social reality of today? There is a tension, clearly, between these two.

What are the next steps? To teach people to solve problems? To have ideas of development? Or to think with people to solve their problems – and to suffer with them, when we meet problems that cannot be solved? One of the great disappointments of social work is that you come daily upon problems that cannot be solved today. You can pass over it and say: 'Oh, that's not my question.' But you can also try to suffer with those who are in the problems that can't be solved today. And with that we come again to our beginning.

Social life – working in social life – is a way to develop abilities which could be used, which could be of value, in coming into the realm of the etheric Christ. Sense of emptiness, dissatisfaction with given explanations, feeling an inner duality – these are the signs of an inner split between what we ought to be able to do and what we are able to do. What we can do is very little. We have to work and work and work for the next little step. There you stand with your beautiful ideas of the end, of the total end, which is so far away. We would like to bring prople on a short-cut to that beautiful end. But it is not worthwhile looking for short-cuts in development. In development, each step has to be done, one after the other. We have to develop the courage to suffer from this duality, and bear it.

At the beginning and at the end, we shall have to develop the new morale – universal pity and compassion with all human beings that suffer from materialism.

Group Life

When working together, one objective can be study. The subject matter of the study is the thing striven after most. This may be a group pursuit. If someone is interested in a thing, of course, he can study it alone. But he may want to deepen his study. He may want to enter it in a deeper way; so he looks for other people who are also interested, and then they study together. They get farther than when each studies alone. Such a group clearly works on a conceptual level – on a level of intellectual content.

Second, we have social groups – the interaction groups. People come together not to study, but to meet each other. The group meets to get acquainted, to have a good time, or to help each other. In the social group it is not subject matter, not what is said, but the interaction that counts.

A third possibility is the action group. The action group sets up aims outside the group. This is a working group. They may be teachers who want to run a Waldorf School. They may run a farm or make a garden. They want to do something which is not just inside the group, but outside, in the world.

In a group of ten people, for instance, let's say there are three who want to work, three who want to study, and four who want to meet each other. This group is not likely to get on well. For group life, people must agree on the character of their group. What is the goal? Is each person's objective the same as that of the group?

The study group, the social group, and the action group – all three have their place and significance.

Firstly, in a group, expectations of different people must meet on the same level. It is better to speak about it in the first half hour than to proceed on different levels of aspiration and expectation. No sound and really good group life develops if the members have conflicting group goals.

Secondly, what are the laws for working in the kind of group chosen? Different laws pertain to the life of groups depending on whether it is a study group, a social group, or an action group.

People mostly don't bother about that. They just go on. They come together and say, 'Let us study', or 'Let us be social', or 'Let us be active'. However, when people meet and say, 'Let us do something', the laws governing their group action must be known. They are different from laws governing group study.

Thirdly – a very awkward thing – when the aims of a group change, is everyone aware of the change? Is everyone willing to enter the new group situation? Often a group starts out as a pure study group, then shifts. About 40 per cent of the members form a social group, whereas 20 per cent want to enter action, and the other 40 per cent still think they are a study group. Much tension, dissatisfaction, and quarrelling stems from the fact that the group began on one level and then shifted. No one was aware of it.

What can we learn and achieve in the different groups?

Group life and group work is a way to practical, karmic understanding. Each meeting with other people is a practical exercise in karma. Who am I? Who is the other?

Steiner, following the Christmas Foundation ceremony, said: 'Anthroposophy ought to lead into practical exercises in karma.' He didn't mean people to go home and shut themselves up in their little room and meditate about former lives – that way illusions will surely enter the soul. Practical exercise in karma means meeting others, because other persons tell me who I am. Steiner taught that even the initiate cannot look into his own incarnations. Other people have to reveal them to him. In meeting other people, a person's own way, his own stream, becomes clearer and clearer.

Let us consider first the study group. Steiner says study is the first step on 'the path of knowledge'. Study is the first step of inner development. When trying to take this first step, it is wise to do it in a group, if one can be found. It is useful to meet another person 'interested with me' in the same subject. Say I am interested, for example, in Chartres, the Cathedral. Say I find other people who are also interested. We then say, 'Let us come together to study it.' Studying together is satisfying and gives everyone 'something to take home' that he couldn't find were he studying alone. That is a gift. But there is a danger. When study is the goal, each member of the group is more or less ego-directed. Each member wants to get something out of the group evening. Each member wants to go home with some new insight. Each member wants to understand things better than before.

Nevertheless, study is a preparation. It is a first step. Before becoming social in spiritual life, before being able to give, something must be accumulated. One cannot give what one does not have. One has to accumulate insight and real spiritual knowledge. One has to study. After studying, one can take the next step. One can give something to other people.

Another danger of the study group is 'intellectual egotism'. This may mean the gobbling up of more and more lectures, yet still not getting enough. More and more – a danger of intellectualism, and an unsatisfying situation. 'I already know something, but I would like to know all things under the stars.' This can be true of people working in a study group, and one should guard against this intellectual egotism.

The lecture group is one where things are so divided that one member speaks and the others listen. That's also a form of study. Although lectures can't be avoided, one should be wary of them. They are worthwhile, for when someone has worked on a subject for many years, he can tell about it to a group of interested people. But when lectures are pedantic, or are faked up, then difficulty arises over the vanity of the lecturer.

Where a group has the lecture habit this occurs: the audience, the public, or the members who are listening, grow in a certain way passive. They become, so to speak, a consumers' league, not a working group. In anthroposophical life, for example, there are old groups who have been together for thirty years each Tuesday evening. They have read lectures and listened to someone explaining the meanings. When asked to become active, or to discuss a problem, they encounter great stress and many difficulties.

The positive aspect of lectures is that they give the possibility to hear in condensed form the work of someone who has researched a subject for many years. The audience receives what lives in the other soul and which the other soul has worked out.

One of the things younger members of the Anthroposophical Society in Holland say is: 'When we come into the groups, nobody greets us. We try to find a chair, we sit down, and we feel very lonely. The lectures are interesting, then we go home. We feel ice cold in a social way, although very much inspired in the intellectual or spiritual way. But we are empty in the region of the heart.' In such a case, something must be done.

In Holland a group of members tried to be aware if new persons came in, and to speak to them, asking them questions, and introducing them. Steiner thought it very important that people should be received – met by someone who goes forward and talks to them. In the Waldorf School, on parents' evening, he always nominated what he called a 'Smiling Committee'. He just said, 'You and you and you will be the Smiling Committee this evening.' That meant a member stood there, greeted the parents, said some nice words, brought them to their place, and gave them a feeling of welcome. This is no empty thing; it is a thing of real life.

One positive thing of group life is learning that another member studies in quite a different way. The other has other interests, feels other values, seeks other ways. One widens one's own horizon when in a group. When one sees how the same content or the same lecture are studied in such totally different ways, it is not worth fighting for the 'right' methods. Fighting for the 'right' methods is doing what old Tobias did. Old Tobias was always right. He always had the 'right' method, and he became blind. He became blind to what was around him. If one only says, 'My method is the only right method, and all the other methods are not right methods', then one gets blind for what is going on in the surroundings.

For the study group, what is the inner way? The inner way of the study group is the eightfold path which works on the sixteen-petalled lotus flower. This is the way of Buddha. The eight things which must be worked on in the eightfold path are: THE RIGHT IMAGE; THE RIGHT JUDGEMENT; THE RIGHT WORD; THE RIGHT ACTION; THE RIGHT STANDPOINT; THE RIGHT OBJECTIVE; THE RIGHT REMEMBRANCE; THE RIGHT OVERALL SURVEY.

The eightfold path, in the overall perspective, means to find *the right balance between the soul and the world.*

Steiner worked with young people. Some groups of young people in Germany, in 1923, went to Steiner and said: 'We have formed our groups of young students, Dr. Steiner, how shall we work together?' Steiner said: 'For God's sake, no lectures!' 'But what shall we do if we can't have lectures?' 'Just speak about your occult experiences.' 'Yes,' they said, 'but we are young people. How can we speak about our occult experiences? We don't have them, Dr. Steiner.' Steiner said: 'Yes, you have them daily. You just pass them by.'

To meet a person and see he is a human being is the first step of Imagination. Without Imagination one can't see if someone is a statue or a living being. Perhaps he moves. But when he doesn't move, one looks in his eyes and sees he is an ego. He is a person. Or when we say, 'This person is sad', or, 'This person is happy' – that is by the force of Imagination.

One can only have deeper Imaginations about the working of the spiritual world into the physical world so that it appears as an image when one has found this right balance. When that right balance isn't there, Imagination becomes just an illusion. One thinks one is seeing something, but the soul and the world are simply out of balance.

Going the eightfold path means *practice* in the ways of the eightfold path – practice in just such a group of people who study. Such a group enters into discussion during study, so that one says, 'Yes, I just read a sentence by Steiner. I understand it in this way.' He tries to describe how he understands it. The other one says: 'I understand it in quite another way.' Don't say: 'You are not right.' Only say, 'I understand it in quite another way. Let us recognize these two standpoints.'

Real Imagination is only built up when one has gone quite around the object of study and has found at least twelve standpoints from which to look at this object of study. At least twelve, Steiner said. In a group of twelve there could be a possibility that all twelve standpoints will be there. When the group is bigger, there is still more chance. This is the challenge: to think, 'I understood it' – and then to hear from another one that he understood it in quite another way. That's the fruit of group study.

The second kind of group is the social group. It consists of personal interaction. The work is not on the subject matter, but *on the group itself*. How is this possible?

I shall tell you how I learned this from a group of young people about thirty years ago. I was not very group-minded. I liked to know things. I liked to study. I had a scientific interest but was not very much interested in other people. In a loose way, yes; but not really.

I thought I was getting on very well in anthroposophy, and then I met a group of young people who were working together in, for me, a quite queer way. They were a mixed group of people. There were students of different faculties, people who were working. One was a clerk in a post office. There was one girl who was not exactly feeble-minded but, you could call it, a borderline case. They were all working together. They were studying from Goethe the metamorphosis of plants.

The first Sunday of each month they came together the whole day. Early, they did eurythmy together. Then they worked on the plants. Then they went on an outing and tried to find plants and look at them and see what were the forces of light, what were the forces of chemical ether, what were the forces of life ether. In the afternoon they returned and studied something else.

When one member of the group didn't understand the thing, they stopped. They said, 'We can't go on when this one hasn't understood it.'

The one slow girl was often the one who didn't understand. Most groups would be keen to get rid of her. She very much hampered the group. But the group didn't do that. They said: 'When we lose one of our members, the group has gone. A convoy doesn't go faster than the slowest ship. We have to stop for the slowest ship and to stay together.'

They asked me once in a while to come with them and to speak about several things, about plants – and I had to study this field. At first, I was really irritated by this way of working. I didn't want to go again. But then, more and more, I saw something happen. I saw a sphere of morality grow in this group, and I saw this girl blossom and come out of her shyness. She went on and she studied. She did her examination as a kindergarten teacher, and she is now very successful. For nearly twenty-five years she has been one of the most successful kindergarten teachers in our country. People come to her to look at how she does it. Why?

In such a group a certain kind of morality arises. The group really carries on for one another. Their first priority was not studying. Studying plants was just the vehicle. They wanted to be a group. They wanted to help each other. They wanted to make progress in the problems of social life.

When building up a social group, members may get dependent on each other. Most people don't like that. But members also become aware of each other.

When becoming aware of another person, what does one see? What does one encounter first? The first things to be seen are the education he or she had, the history of life, the feelings, the strivings. When getting acquainted more deeply with some person, one bumps into the old karma of the other person.

What is present in the sheaths – the physical, etheric, and

astral body of someone – is the history of life, of this life, and the history of former lives. What does it mean to bump into the 'double' of another person? In a social context, the first thing one grows aware of is the old Adam and the old Eve. All in the person that comes from former lives and from the history of this life. The 'double' is just the contraction of this old karma.

But one has to learn to look behind the 'double', and to ask 'What does the ego strive for behind that "double"?' The 'double' can seem a little queer. One says, 'Oh, I don't want to get acquainted with such a person.' Then one learns to know him really. One can practise, in such a group, looking through, or behind, the 'double'. There one finds the striving ego – the ego striving to develop a future, a higher situation, a higher life.

When people live a long time together in a close situation and each day have to be together, this 'bumping of doubles' can become a kind of psychosis. People get quite psychotic as a result of each other. We call it in psychiatry 'submarine psychosis'. When people have to live together, twenty or thirty men in very narrow quarters, the way someone does this or that little thing irritates one, so that one says, 'If you don't stop, I'll kill you.' When one meets something like that in life, it means to bump into the 'double' of another person. What is irritating is not the striving ego, but the old Adam, the 'double', something 'fixed'. It is always doing the same thing, always saying the same thing, always acting in the same way. In group life, one can practise the following as an exercise: 'Now I want to know those ten people we are working with.' It doesn't mean going into their private life and asking intimate questions. By asking so-called intimate questions one always comes on the 'double' again.

Try to find the point where this person speaks out of his ego. What does he really want to achieve in life? Where are his deepest longings? When one knows them, one knows something about that other – about the ego of the other person as a striving person. Trying to get in touch with the ego of the other person brings out the beautiful fruits that come from social group life.

Of course, there are very great dangers of clique-building, of sentimentality, of irritation, oppression, hatred, and withdrawal of certain people. In the United States people don't like to go into these difficulties. They like to keep things nice and warm and not go into nastiness, but just live in a way so as not to be irritated by the other.

What are the special qualities to learn in the social group? In the social group we can enter on what Steiner called the six-fold path, the development of the twelve-petalled lotus flower. This is in the heart. Steiner says the sixfold path is the Christian path of modern times. What is the sixfold path? To sum it up: CONTROL OF THINKING; CONTROL OF DOING; ENDURANCE AND EVENNESS; TOLERANCE (POSITIVITY AND IMPARTIALITY); AND UNCONCERNEDNESS OR DISINTERESTEDNESS.

And as the sixth element, for balance of the soul: QUIET UNDERSTANDING. That is the goal and fruit of the sixfold path.

Quiet understanding. That means to be able to understand the other person – there must be quietness in one's heart. One's soul must be quiet so that one can perceive what is going on in the other soul. The great way of development for modern mankind is, Steiner says, the sixfold path, which has to be followed now. The eightfold path was the path of Buddha; the sixfold path is the path of the modern man.

Developing these qualities is a way of developing social skills. It is the way of developing moral phantasy (moral Imagination). It is a way of developing *Inspiration.* Being aware of the ego behind the 'double' of the other one is already a step on the path of Inspiration. When one looks at a child, and one loves the child, one can love just the beautiful hair, the nice voice, the soft skin. But one can also learn to love the ego which is behind the child and which is striving towards unfolding. This is already a step on the way of Inspiration. No teacher can be a good teacher without having developed a certain degree of Inspiration. That's the great gift of people who have to work with children.

The third kind of group is the action group, or the initiative group. This group comes together to take initiative or to take action. When can a group be an action group? Not merely when ten or twenty people are entering into action. An action group is a group of people that are already a group. An action group must first be a group. That means to find some way – by study, by practice, or by the development of social skills – to be a group, and then this group is able to set an objective in the world. When the group is willing to set an objective in the world, it can then be an instrument for social building. The Hierarchies can enter in. It can be an organism of the spiritual world. An action group – one that is really a group – can be an organism of the spiritual world.

When a group, potentially an organism of the spiritual world, has overcome the old karmic forces, it strives to look at each other's spiritual egos in the group. It strives to develop what the other one in his spiritual ego wants, not what his various sheaths want. This is a real action group working out of *Intuition*. Hierarchies may then work through the group; the group becomes an instrument of the Hierarchies.

The ego stands in it; but the group acts out of Intuition. New karma is built. This new karma is Sun karma. The old karma is Moon karma. It came through the gate of the Moon into earthly life. The old karma forces are arranged so that they enter life with the person who is being born. That is his old karma, a Moon karma. But during life, started by the activity of his ego, he is building up a new Sun karma. This radiates out to the future; it is that karma which, in lives hereafter, will develop. This is the path of developing the ten-petalled lotus flower: the fivefold path.

In KNOWLEDGE OF THE HIGHER WORLDS, Steiner speaks about this ten-petalled lotus flower, and the fivefold path which leads into the future. The sixfold path leads into the social life. It has to do with interpersonal relations in the life now and here. The fivefold path leads into the future.

What is the fivefold path? The first step is to learn to command sense perceptions. The second is to control 'fancies' – to control them and ask, 'Where do they come from?' Thirdly, in our whole life, we experience a great deal of unconscious perception, coming to us through our ears, through our eyes, but also through the magnetic forces out of the earth. We have to build up a soul armour against unconscious perceptions. Fourthly, avoid accepting things without thinking. One hears all sorts of things, and one relaxes and reads the paper. All kinds of things are accepted without thinking. We have to learn to live so that things which come in must be clear and in such a form that one has to think about them. Then, putting these four together, Steiner added: *Severe self-discipline*.

This means that people who are in an action group have to find a way to 'give in'. They have to accept the other as the other is and give positive possibilities room to work.

Each member has to keep the negative forces to himself and he must work on them in his own little room.

Putting these things together, then: we have old karma – old karma is all the things that we know and can do. That we can do and know, that we have abilities, that we have knowledge –

all that comes out of old karma. We have the meeting, the encountering of other people, and taking the other into one's own life. We can't know another person when we have not taken this person into our own life and made him a part of it. Then the new karma comes through our will.

This is karma for the future.

One can speak of groups in this way:
– In the *study group*, old karma reveals itself.
– In the *social group*, old karma is rearranged.
– In the *action group,* new karma is formed.

Practically, then, when working in a group, ask yourself: 'What is the objective of this group? What are we doing? Is the group aware of what it is doing? Is everyone on the same level of expectation?'

Systems, Levels, and Threefoldness

How, in today's social reality, do we go about realizing approaches to Rudolf Steiner's concept of the Threefold Commonwealth?

There are two directions, when engaged in study, to work in. The first of these is to study current social and world problems. In such a study we have to consider three levels of the problems:
– the level of eternal spiritual ideas.
– the level of sensible social concepts.
– the level of the social reality of the practical situation.

There is a second study approach. The need for this arises when we think of actually trying, in a new way, to live in groups. If we do this with the goal of trying to realize one or another aspects of the Threefold Commonwealth principles, then we must study these principles themselves – again remembering the three levels of the problem.

Both these directions need to be followed. In the first, we survey the world and its problems with principles of the Threefold Commonwealth in mind. In the second, we study the principles of the Threefold Commonwealth in order to build a community along such lines.

A third direction, which is in a certain sense a corollary to both the above directions, or a synthesis of the two, is that of bringing threefold action – that is action living out of the threefold principles – into the world. This can be done out of a study of current world social problems, or it can be done out of community work aimed at realizing aspects of the threefold principles.

To study the principles of the Threefold Commonwealth, we have first to turn to the lectures and books of Steiner. In these lectures, which were held between 1919 and 1922, the material deals with the level of spiritual ideas. These eternal spiritual ideas are in the lectures, in the books, and also in the whole of anthroposophy. The Threefold Commonwealth stands against the whole background of anthroposophy with its concepts of the threefold man, the threefold social life, the threefold hierarchical life, and, supremely, the concept of the Trinity. The Holy Trinity stands supreme.

In threefold hierarchical life, in the threefold constitution of man, and in the threefold formation of the social life, we meet eternal spiritual ideas.

But in the lectures and books on the Threefold Commonwealth, given in 1919 and 1920, we meet literature which is only partially about eternal ideas. Here Steiner is already going on into the second field, that of sensible social concepts. He speaks about them out of the situation of about 1920. These sensible social concepts are *in between* eternal spiritual ideas on the one side, and on the other side the social reality of the moment. The social reality, moreover, is bound to a situation of a certain period. It is always changing and developing.

Thus, to arrive at sensible social concepts, we have first to look and work upon the eternal spiritual ideas. We have also to know about the social reality of the present. Then we ask: 'Well, what are the workable, sensible social concepts now?' We have to create them anew.

However, from Steiner's work in the years 1919–20 we can learn one thing. We can look historically at the social reality and situation of 1920 and observe a methodological example of how to translate eternal spiritual ideas into sensible social concepts – as it was done then.

Going about this in such a way develops methodical thinking in the field of threefold social life.

Next, when we ask what would be sensible social concepts for now, we have to look at the development of social reality since 1920. Not only the problems which were there in 1920 still count, but a realm exists of quite new situations not known in the twenties. We have to bring this knowledge together with that of the eternal spiritual ideas.

One view of recent developments arises from a survey of materialism in the 19th and 20th centuries. Materialism in the 19th century was materialism in thinking; materialism in the 20th century is materialism in practice. In the 19th century materialistic thinking was built up by those enthusiastic scientists who from 1850 on until the end of the century, and in the beginning of this century, until the end of the First World War, worked on materialistic concepts of the world. This materialistic thinking already meant a kind of new crucifixion of the Christ.

Materialism in practice is an even greater cross for the spiritual world.

This is materialism that has entered the will. How has it developed since 1920? In the will, materialism means the practical construction of the world anew. This construction of a new world in the technical field is done through knowledge of physical laws. In social life it is done through programming life into the future through social models. This materialism has developed along practical lines especially quickly since 1945. The last world war speeded up the work of Ahriman both in thinking and in practice.

The new thing since the last world war is systems analysis. Since 1945, we have been able to build systems of self-sustaining forces. They are called closed systems. A closed system results when forces work together with so-called feed-back which keeps these forces within a field out of which they cannot go.

One of the most simple examples of closed system is the heating system in houses. The system moves between a set minimum and maximum. The temperature stays within a degree or so of the point at which the needle is set. A needle set at 72 degrees Fahrenheit will keep the temperature constant between $70\frac{1}{2}$ and $73\frac{1}{2}$ degrees. The temperature goes up, but as soon as it reaches $73\frac{1}{2}$ degrees, the feed-back from the heating system – in this case the higher room temperature – triggers the thermostat which turns the furnace off momentarily. The temperature goes down. The furnace turns back on when the temperature dips again to $70\frac{1}{2}$ degrees.

This is a very simple closed system. This system is closed by the feed-back of information from outside the heating components – the temperature of the room as read by the thermostat.

Men are now able to build much more complex closed systems. In a sense, they are copies of Ahrimanic imitations of living organisms. The secret of life, in the Ahrimanic world, is such a closed system. It is patterned after the single cell which can hold its own salts together even if introduced into water with salt, or without salt. We call something like the single cell a stable system. The grade of stability of a closed system depends on how it is built. It can be built with more or less tolerance. The factors which are put into a system are called variables. In the example of heating, the variable is temperature, but not humidity. After choosing the variable to incorporate into the system, a control is built in order to close the variable within the system. Systems can be built for one or two variables, but there are also systems with ten or twenty variables. Then they get very complex and can only be handled with higher mathematics. Specialists have to handle such systems.

Systems can be built and assigned a specified kind of 'behaviour'. We can then, in the jargon, call for a closed system with this or that 'behaviour'. These are called input/output systems.

Look at schools. They can be set up as input/output systems. The school is like the heating system. The children are like the rooms to be heated. A curriculum may be viewed as the school input. And so on.

This is one of the greatest things Ahriman brought to mankind in the last twenty years – the concept of the input/output system.

What is done with this in agriculture? In agriculture the crop on the field is looked at as an input/output system. Seeds go in, plants come out. What minerals are being taken by the plant out of the soil? There is an output of the soil, so there will have to be an input. The soil too has to be an input/output system. So and so much chemical fertilizer has to go in to balance so much element gone out. And so on.

In psychology since the beginning of this century there has been a so-called stimulus response model. This school of psychology maintains that the human being is a closed system of forces. At the beginning it is a system of forces with no content, a child at birth. I remember one of the best books on psychology written in the United States starts with the following sentence: 'The problem of education is the problem of how protoplasm meets society.' Protoplasm is a closed system. A living cell is a closed system. The whole human being is therefore viewed as an input/output system on these lines. That means something has to go in for something to come out later. This view becomes the great psychological background of the whole modern educational edifice which says, 'The child is born as a biological being, a closed system of forces; to have output, there will have to be input.' As John Locke said in the 17th century, 'All things that are in men have come through the senses. Nothing comes that has not come through the senses.' The whole of modern psychology and of modern education lives in this Lockian tradition.

Lockian thinking is already patterned like an input/output model.

Everywhere this output/input thinking can be found. We find it when we look at ourselves and our thinking. It is an infectious disease. We are all in one way or another thinking in input/output models, also when we try to work in anthroposophy. We have to fight it to the last. Just when we think we have overcome it it comes back on a higher field. We begin thinking of the work of the Hierarchies from Saturn to Vulcan as an input/output model. We ask ourselves, 'What was the input at the beginning of Saturn, and what will be the output at the end?' Who of us has not asked what will become of mankind at the end of Vulcan? Such questions cannot be asked. There is freedom in this field. Even the highest initiate cannot tell what the world will be like within twenty years.

In the last twenty years this input/output model thinking has said: 'Yes, there are always forces and variables outside the model.' Humidity is just such a variable outside of the model of a heating system. Such a force outside of the model is called a parameter.

In the psychological input/output model of people, the human being is pictured as being totally blank at the beginning and filled with wisdom at the end. But in this input/output model, the ego – the spiritual ego – is a parameter. In the input/output models of stimulus and response, the closed system works thus: 'I am hungry. I have to eat. I am satisfied. I am hungry again. I eat again. I am satisfied.' In this closed system of hunger, eating, and satisfaction, *the ego of man is a spiritual parameter*. It is a force from outside the stimulus response field.

Parameters are often considered obstacles, because they spoil the beautiful model. There is, after all, a *man* in this beautiful model of getting hungry, eating, getting hungry again. There is a man who says, 'I am getting hungry. I have to eat. But first I have to write that letter.' He does *not* eat. He faces hunger and goes outside of the circle, because from outside there came a force of another quality than the force within the system. These parameters are great *crooks* to the modern system and model builders.

This was the point of the example given in chapter two of the economists who wanted advice about school education in Nigeria. They wanted to know how much money should be invested in education to have, over the years, so and so many people at the level of primary education, so and so many ready for higher education, and so and so many at the level of university education. They did not ask which methods of education to use. No. They only wanted to know how much money should be invested in it. After a study of this, with all things going through the computers in the modern way, they had a model for the relationship between investment and output of qualified younger people.

However, there are parameters in this field – sometimes called cultural obstacles. One such obstacle in some cultures is that an intellectual does not work. This is an awful obstacle to the models for investment.

I told them out of my own experience in the Orient another thing. 'When investing money in education, you will get a crop of young university people out of the country in which you are doing this work. This will be the kernel of the new revolution. These are the people who will start the new revolutions, because they have a university education. They have to work in a culture which is not up to a level to be able to use these people in the right way. Since they do not find things going their way, they become the revolutionaries for the next generation. This also is an obstacle to model investments. 'Tell us,' they asked, 'how much money do we have to put in to overcome these obstacles?' I answered: 'You cannot do this with money. You can only do it by sending people who have a heart that really beats with the needs of their culture. You will have to educate this whole culture. Change means a whole generation. The culture has to be changed so that the education is something that is inside the culture and not outside the culture.' 'Oh, yes, we understand, but how much does that *cost*?'

I asked: 'Why are you always thinking in money? Why are you not thinking what *method* of education you need to help the people of Nigeria to come up to the level of the conscious soul?' I did not say the words 'consciousness soul'. I used another word.

'No, that is impossible,' they said, 'that is outside of our model. We have no place for that in our model. Our model has to be a money model just as our heating system is a temperature model. We want to bring everything under one thing: that is money.'

Here I have simplified a little bit, but this was a very tense discussion. They grew very angry with me because I always said there are variables, parameters to the system. They cannot be tackled with money alone. This input/output thinking tries to reduce all problems in the world to one factor, to one variable.

These are not just brutish people who are only thinking in money. These are university assistants, mathematicians, and other trained people who gain little money with the work they are doing. They could go into industry and earn much more. But they say, 'No, we want to do a real social work, and for this real social work we want to build up a model.'

One of my colleagues is a world-famous man. He was invited to the United States as a professor. He says: 'We are now so far along that the economy of man can be reduced to five factors, to five variables. With these five variables we can run the economy of the whole world.' I said to him: 'Happy for the world. We may be happy that the world asked you to do this because the economy may run according to your model. But you will find out there are many parameters you did not think about.'

At the time of Rudolf Steiner in 1920 there was no idea about this kind of problem of social models. There was no idea that this was a real social issue. Now it has become a social issue of the first order. And when we are building a social model now, we have to make our choice of *which* factors, *which* variables we want to include. We can only overcome materialism in this field when we put stress upon the parameters. You could go and fight these people by saying, 'The models are wrong.' But within the field of selected variables the models may be right. There is no fighting them. Only by pointing at parameters, by pointing at forces coming out of another level, can a contribution be made.

When speaking with psychologists in the Lockean tradition, I try to bring into the discussion the parameter of the ego and the parameter of personal freedom. This is an awful parameter for them, because out of freedom, out of the ego, comes the force of free choice. Free choice always spoils the model. The ego is the great revolutionary in social life. Our astral body is in reality an etheric-astral constitution, a model into which are built a great many forces working quite automatically. This constitution is a closed model. Then a parameter comes in, the human ego. The ego uses this model for another thing than for what it was built for. The ego unbends the model, loosening the system from the pattern of the model itself.

We can try to overcome materialism in agriculture in the biodynamic gardening method by showing that with an input/output method of chemical fertilization, forces remain outside of the model. The chemical fertilizers are the input, the plants are the output – but what about the forces which are outside the models?

Think about medicines which are treated through a rhythm. Homeopathy cannot be understood from the input/output point of view, because the opponents say, 'You must put in what comes out. But you never put a new thing in. You dilute a grain of substance one to ten, then dilute it again. All things are disappearing and there is nothing left. Just water.'

To counter this argument one has to point to the parameter of rhythm. The rhythms work on the medicaments. The rhythm is from outside the input/output system Without having done a great deal of work on the influence of rhythm and the real essence of rhythm, one cannot offset the materialistic view of medicines given us.

To heal social life, healing has to be brought to these system builders.

The human ego comes in to the psychological model. The physical, etheric, and astral aspects of man may be bound by laws that make a closed system, but then the ego enters with its karma, with its own objectives, and with its own possibilities. This ego comes out of another world, outside the system of a human being as he is when looked at only as an astral body. Development of freedom and freedom of choice lie outside of the stimulus/response field, outside the input/output model of the world. In this world of models, with his ego, man has the freedom of choice to pose new variables, new factors from outside.

There is a great danger even when trying to understand Rudolf Steiner – and I have this problem to fight in myself day after day – that we take the Threefold Commonwealth as a closed model. Everything works beautifully in this model. If people would only accept the beautiful model of the Threefold Commonwealth all things would go as they should, we say. When thinking this way, we are still thinking in the way of Ahriman, in the world of the model. In social life there is one great parameter, a force outside this whole field: that is Christ. Christ enters to bring the possibility of freedom to man. In social life, this is the force of love. The force of love can be an obstacle for the social system builders. For the force of love is a force outside of economic and social systems which makes the impossible possible.

Love introduces a factor which cannot be accounted for.

Ahrimanic thinking says, 'It costs so and so much money to hire so many people who have love.' But love is not for hire. Man can live out of freedom, and he can bring love, and the whole system changes.

The only possibility of evolution is to bring into this world of automatic growth the new outside force of love. Love makes it possible to work in social life. After the first step of studying the thing, and we then try to live in a threefold social life, we can only live and be really human in such a social life when we not only know the laws of social life, but when we bring to these laws the parameter of love.

We also face the problem of really *doing* in social life. We then have to work out of our ego forces. The ego forces are forces which we brought, with our karma, according to our special personal possibilities.

The first step is to take Threefold Commonwealth thinking as an Imagination: an Imagination of eternal spiritual ideas. We are in the field of Imagination when building up an image of what Steiner brought to us as the eternal spiritual ideas out of the great mystery of the Trinity in the form of the threefold social life.

But then entering into social life to realize a certain kind of possibility – one of the very many possibilities of real threefold social life – then we can only do this out of the forces of Inspiration. Inspiration means that we are inspired, that something from outside comes into what we are doing. That is the human ego. In the human ego works the force of the Christ which brings the force of love. This can change the whole model.

At another level comes the work of bringing the threefold method of handling problems into the world. This is doing. We can only do this out of the force of Intuition. Intuition means that something comes into my ego which goes towards the future.

There are great dangers now which we have to fight, and we have to try to live and to think the Threefold Commonwealth as Steiner taught us. One danger is the force of Lucifer who influences the people who are the central regulation makers. Lucifer tries to enter into social life to make a closed system of regulations from a centralized point. That was what Steiner fought against in the twenties, because, in the twenties, came to mankind a new kind of thinking having a complete model of social life, centrally regulated, so that it runs like a good machine.

But on the other side we have to fight another force, too. We have to fight the Ahrimanic model builders which were not there in the twenties. So we have on the one side still to fight the regulation makers, and we have on the other side a much stronger fight, a much more difficult fight, to fight against model makers in the modern world. This model thinking is the greatest enemy of threefold thinking. When you see what these model builders can achieve at the moment, what the central regulation makers are doing is child's work in comparison. What model builders will bring now and in the near future into our social life, forcing people to go into model systems in factories, model systems in administration departments, model systems in school life, in teaching and so on, we hardly imagine. They will bring us a model for each thing we have to do. They will always reduce it to one or two factors. One of the factors will always be money. The other factor will be power. Money and power are the factors they are looking for.

So we have quite a new field to deal with in addition to that which Steiner already faced.

Steiner taught a great many sensible social concepts. They are in his lectures and in his books. There were tensions with the beginning of socialism and the tendency towards social regulation – but now we have to fight quite another force which will go much more into our private secret life, and which wants us to have all things done after a model. Eating according to a model, getting children according to a model, building a school according to a model, educating according to a model, paying taxes according to a model.

We can only overcome these tendencies when we are aware of them – of these model builders in science, in psychology, in social life, in the economy, in politics, and so on. When we are aware of them, we know that we can't fight them in their own field. Ahriman is much too clever.

The only thing you can do, just at the end, when a very clever model is put before you, is to show the forces which are working from outside the factory, for example, that they have selected for their model. Point to the parameters. Then, as a human being, stress the ego. In bio-dynamic or medical work, stress something like rhythm as a reality.

To all things which are regulated and modelled, to all systems which in coming years try to force life into rigid social patterns, stress love as the parameter.

Towards the 21st Century

Christ's life wrote into the Earth a new rhythm – a rhythm of $33\frac{1}{3}$ years. That was the time from the birth in Bethlehem until the Easter on Golgotha. This rhythm of Christ's life on Earth is the rhythm of the social work of modern man. Development, in Christian times, and more and more now, shows impulses Christianized out of the will, working on the social life of man in this rhythm of years. Something in the will now comes from outside later as a kind of resurrection.

Steiner always speaks about this third of a century rhythm; the outer world knows about this already.

The old mysteries before Christ were mysteries of wisdom and beauty; the new mysteries are mysteries of love and development. Development and love are mysteries of the will – they are mysteries of the heart. Look at what happened in the world in the first third of this century. There stood a great initiate of mankind in the Sun mysteries, Rudolf Steiner. He brought impulses of renewal for art and for development. Only a small group of men took up these first beginnings of a new era. They studied. They made foundations and beginnings and sought to do something with these impulses.

The second third of the century, the middle third, started at Easter 1933. What was the task then? The anthroposophical movement, now without its leader, should have been the bearer of the new Sun mysteries, able to work the forces of the etheric Christ into the needs of mankind.

This was the greatest event to happen in the 20th century. We were there. Our task was to take this event as a reality into our hearts and to work with it throughout the second third of this century.

In 1924, after the Christmas Foundation ceremony, Steiner gave two cycles of lectures for medical students and young doctors. He gave them a task: 'Write an essay. It need not be more than five pages. A small essay upon how you think the world will be in 1935.'

They responded as best they could. Steiner was very sad about these answers. He said they were beautiful in development, in positive forces, but absolutely blind to the working of the counter forces. They did not reckon with the counter forces which would work against such an event as the coming of the etheric Christ. They had forgotten that the forces of darkness would not be still, would not be silent. When such a thing happens as the etheric resurrection of Christ, all the forces of darkness gather together and try to plan how to prevent mankind from seeing. The young people of 1924 were enthusiastic about things which were going on then. They developed the positive things in a beautiful way. But they had forgotten one thing: the forces of darkness. And that was a great failure of anthroposophical work in the second third of this century.

There can be no real start in the last third of the century without the courage to look out in an objective way. What happened in the second part of this century? The forces of darkness knew about the happening of the appearance of Christ in the etheric world. They made so much noise and put so much stress on mankind that people could not hear what really was going on. In January 1933, Hitler came to power in Germany. He made so much noise that everyone was transfixed like little birds who look at snakes and can't move.

In the Anthroposophical Society, after the death of Steiner, the forces of unity failed. The society split. The Anthroposophical Society was lamed for its task. It could only go on working as well as possible, in small groups, and try to make the best of it. There were warm hearts beating for spiritual reality. But as a whole, we must look back upon this period and see it as it is.

Why say these things? Why not be pleasant and not speak about it? Because there are new forces at work. New possibilities exist in the last third of the century. In the anthroposophical world, impulses exist for coming together. That is a positive aspect.

There also work in the culture in the outside world other forces. This last part of the century can be seen in two ways. It can be seen as the period in which the great battle between Ahriman and Michael will climax. To set before you a positive picture, I will repeat what I presented at the start of chapter two. Steiner, in the years after 1920, wrote letters to a certain widow, a widow of a Society member who died at the end of the First World War. He gave her advice on how to live with the dead. He told her what was going on in the consciousness of her husband who had died. These letters still exist. By good fortune I met the daughter of this widow. She read me parts out of these letters.

Steiner told how the one who has gone through the gates of death wakes up, looks down on the earth, and comes to the following Imagination. Ahriman sits in a cave under the earth. He works. He writes things down, counting and counting, calculating and calculating. He tries to build up a whole world out of a new mathematics. There, Steiner says, Michael stands beside him waiting. For Michael knows that he will make the final addition.

Such a picture can be a help for the last part of this century. Ahriman is counting and counting and counting, making most beautiful mathematical models of the whole world. At the end Michael, with his sword, will make the sum. This moment has not yet come. Michael is waiting, standing by the side, waiting. He can do this when people on earth are there fighting and going with him.

Ahriman brings his thoughts to the world, in one sphere, through advertising. Consider this advertisement out of the *New York Times,* August 5th, 1965. It is an advertisement of a company that had been thirty years in existence. They brought out a great advertisement for their anniversary called, *Reflections on the Age of Change*. It said:

> Next year the world will enter the final third of the end of the twentieth century. Only one thing about it is certain. It will be almost unimaginably different from all past ages. The middle slice, a little more than a generation, is now drawing to a close. More basic and far reaching changes have taken place in the world during the last thirty years than in the three hundred years preceding those. The age of change is a significant mark in human history. It signifies not merely that there have been many changes, but the rate of change itself has accelerated faster than men ever had dreamed possible. We all know the serious events of the last three decades. The great depression, the Second World War, the rise of new nations, the struggle for power, the spread of affluence, the technological revolution in making and building and distributing beneath this potent march of events. More drastic and perhaps more decisive changes have taken place today. About one out of every twenty-four human beings who ever lived are alive now.

The rate of the world population increase has doubled in this second third of the twentieth century – has doubled in one generation. Seven out of ten medical prescriptions were not known thirty years ago. At that time only one farm out of ten in the United States had commercial electric service and we were still largely a rural nation. Now the urban areas exceed the rural areas in population. Only ten per cent of our citizens supply us with our agricultural needs. The centre of the USA population has shifted steadily westwards. It is now a few miles from the city of Centralia, Illinois. National wealth and power have followed the population westwards. There has been the most enormous knowledge explosion in history. Four times as much is known as in 1935, and in the next fifteen years scientists will know as much as in all previous history. As many scientific papers have been published since 1950 alone as were published in all the centuries before. About 60,000 new products were introduced in the USA last year. There were only 2,000 a year, a decade ago, and only a few hundred a year in the early 1930s. Life has been made incredibly easier for millions. The sheer physical effort of living has been so reduced that minds and bodies have been freed for many more cultural and recreational pursuits than the average man could have hoped for a generation ago. Our gross national product has more than doubled in thirty years. We have an ever growing middle class in which more people have more than ever before. Our explorations in space are dramatic and exciting. Technology can also provide us with better means for living peacefully on earth if we can curb ancient enmities and envies and fears. Now new forms of food products, new forms of energy, new developments in computers and automation, make the last third of our century a flowering of the human spirit. There is unprecedented challenge ahead. There is great promise and deep menace. Our reach into the future can be creative and productive, against profit and disease, against prejudice and ignorance, against those dark elements in our nature that set man against man and nation against nation. Where this last third of this century will take us no one knows, but we do know that we now have the knowledge, the tools, the scientific and industrial potential, to make the world a better place than it ever has been before, as also for making it the worst place. Alfred Whitehead, one of the foremost philosophers of the twentieth century, said shortly before he died: 'The art of progress is to preserve order amid change, and to preserve change amid order.' We pray that the coming age of unknown change will come with order, with love, with cool sanity the world so desperately needs in the years ahead.

Now this is advertising. This is the way Ahriman works. He advertises spiritual truth in his way. And what he has told is the truth. This is one of the ways you can look at the third part of the century, at the next thirty years, with an explosion of knowledge, an explosion of new possibilities, a doubling of the population of the earth.

Now we can take another picture. What did Steiner say of this last part of the century? He gave us the picture of the Michael School since 1500 preparing the people who could stand in the new Sun mysteries. The whole Michael School is coming to the earth towards the end of the century. The great teachers of Chartres and all the people who went to the schools of Plato, the great Dominicans who went to the schools of Aristotle. They will build new forces, parameters in our culture, new forces which are ouside the model Ahriman builds.

Ahriman builds models with just those forces he wants to have in the model. These Michaelic forces are of other qualities. They are outside the model. They are the things which disturb the beautiful model. Ahriman, by advertising, tells us that this last part of the century will be a century of unexpected, positive, earthly possibilities: of an earthly paradise. We know in this beautiful model of Ahriman there are parameters. There are forces of another quality from outside the model. They are the people who have gone through the school of Michael, descending to the earth in this last part of the century. They will bring in forces with which Ahriman has not reckoned, which are outside of the possibilities he could think of.

The force of love is a parameter to the Ahrimanic world. It is a disturbance to the model building of the Ahrimanic world. So is the force of light. The real mysteries of the Mercury forces tried to bring darkness up into light.

They who stand in the school of Michael in the last third of this century will come into a whirlpool of forces. Steiner announces this and says that they who stand in the Michael school will not only live in the world of light and of clear thinking, they will have to dive into a whirlpool of forces: of Ahrimanic forces, Luciferic forces, and Christian light forces. They will have to find their way through this whirlpool. Where is the help?

We help Michael in his struggle with Ahriman by studying spiritual science so that Michael can make the account of the mathematical formulae of Ahriman. That is the first step: studying the world, getting world minded. Michael wants insights that benefit all men alike. Insights which only benefit a small group of people are not wanted. So we need to go out in the world to know about the world. We have to build groups that have an objective task outside the group. We have to do deeds which are not necessarily only out of our old karma but deeds which we *don't* have to do, deeds of freedom.

Many deeds in life must be done out of our own old karma. We have to do many things out of necessity. But in this world we have also to bring in things which have no necessity, no old karma. They are free things for the future.

We have to have courage to work out of spiritual insight. We have to found schools. Things which have been already started, we have to maintain.

Within the model that Ahriman has set, and which he advertises daily, we shall not find the forces to withstand the difficulties and to build a Sun world in our society. But that is just what we have to do. To build small spots of a Sun world in our society.

Outside the model of the world that is advertised by Ahriman, there is a world of light which enlightens the dark caves of Ahriman. There is light coming into the dark cave of Ahriman. Ahriman is blinded. He gets uncertain. And he will be bound to the earth forces where he belongs.

We have to seek for the light forces in our thinking. We have to enter into the sorrow and compassion of the world in our feelings. The etheric Christ creates seed forces with which we may go into the frightful situation of the last part of this century, frightful situations created by Ahriman. But these situations need be without light only for those who are under the spell of Ahriman. For those hearts that beat for Michael, there is nothing totally frightful in the world, no apocalypse without hope.

There is only work to be done; light to be found.

List of works by Rudolf Steiner recommended, among others, for study in conncection with the foregoing lectures:

Knowledge of Higher Worlds and Its Attainment

The Stages of Higher Knowledge

Occult Science — An Outline

A Road to Self Knowledge

Christianity as Mystical Fact

The Etherisation of the Blood

True Nature of the Second Coming

The Spiritual Guidance of Man & Mankind

Three Streams in the Evolution of Mankind

Cosmic Memory

At the Gates of Spiritual Science

Threefold Social Order (The Threefold Commonwealth)

The Social Future

Catalogues and all the published works of Rudolf Steiner now in print in English translation and in the original German, as well as other authors on Anthroposophy can be obtained from Steiner Book Centre, Inc., 151 Carisbrooke Crescent, North Vancouver, Canada V7N 2S2